HISTORIANS AT WORK

What Caused the Pueblo Revolt of 1680?

Readings Selected and Introduced by

David J. Weber

Southern Methodist University

Selections by

Henry Warner Bowden

Ramón A. Gutiérrez

Van Hastings Garner

Angélico Chávez

Andrew L. Knaut

Bedford / St. Martin's   *Boston* ♦ *New York*

For Bedford/St. Martin's

History Editor: Katherine E. Kurzman
Developmental Editor: Jen Lesar
Production Supervisor: Catherine Hetmansky
Marketing Manager: Charles Cavaliere
Copyeditor: Barbara G. Flanagan
Text Design: Claire Seng-Niemoeller
Cover Design: Peter Blaiwas
Cover Art: Fred Kabotie, *1680 Pueblo Revolt at Hopi,* 1976. Courtesy of the Museum of Indian Arts and Culture/Laboratory of Anthropology, Santa Fe
Composition: G&S Typesetters, Inc.
Printing and Binding: Haddon Craftsmen, Inc.

President: Charles H. Christensen
Editorial Director: Joan E. Feinberg
Director of Editing, Design, and Production: Marcia Cohen
Managing Editor: Elizabeth M. Schaaf

Library of Congress Catalog Card Number: 98–87544

Manufactured in the United States of America.

3   2   1   0   9
f   e   d   c   b

For information, write: Bedford/St. Martin's, 75 Arlington Street, Boston, MA 02116 (617-399-4000)

ISBN: 0–312–19174–X

Acknowledgments

Page xi: Map adapted from *The Pueblo Indians of North America* by George Spindler, Edward P. Dozier, and Louise Spindler. Copyright © 1970 by Holt, Rinehart, and Winston. Reproduced by permission of the publisher.

HENRY WARNER BOWDEN, "Spanish Missions, Cultural Conflict, and the Pueblo Revolt of 1680," *Church History* (1975): 217–28. Courtesy of the American Society of Church History.

ANGÉLICO CHÁVEZ, "Pohé-yemo's Representative and the Pueblo Revolt of 1680," *New Mexico Historical Review* 42 (1967): 85–126. Courtesy of the *New Mexico Historical Review.*

VAN HASTINGS GARNER, "Seventeenth Century New Mexico," *Journal of Mexican American History* (1974): 41–70. By permission of Van Hastings Garner.

RAMÓN A. GUTIÉRREZ, from *When Jesus Came, the Corn Mothers Went Away* by Ramón A. Gutiérrez. Reprinted with the permission of the publishers, Stanford University Press. © 1991 by the Board of Trustees of the Leland Stanford Junior University.

ANDREW L. KNAUT, from *The Pueblo Revolt of 1680: Conquest and Resistance in Seventeenth-Century New Mexico* by Andrew L. Knaut. Copyright © 1995 by the University of Oklahoma Press.

It is a violation of the law to reproduce these selections by any means whatsoever without the written permission of the copyright holder.

Foreword

The short, inexpensive, and tightly focused books in the Historians at Work series set out to show students what historians do by turning closed specialist debate into an open discussion about important and interesting historical problems. These volumes invite students to confront the issues historians grapple with while providing enough support so that students can form their own opinions and join the debate. The books convey the intellectual excitement of "doing history" that should be at the core of any undergraduate study of the discipline. Each volume starts with a contemporary historical question that is posed in the book's title. The question focuses on either an important historical document (the Declaration of Independence, the Emancipation Proclamation) or a major problem or event (the beginnings of American slavery, the Pueblo Revolt of 1680) in American history. An introduction supplies the basic historical context students need and then traces the ongoing debate among historians, showing both how old questions have yielded new answers and how new questions have arisen. Following this two-part introduction are four or five interpretive selections by top scholars, reprinted in their entirety from journals and books, including endnotes. Each selection is either a very recent piece or a classic argument that is still in play and is headed by a question that relates it to the book's core problem. Volumes that focus on a document reprint it in the opening materials so that students can read arguments alongside the evidence and reasoning on which they rest.

One purpose of these books is to show students that they *can* engage with sophisticated writing and arguments. To help them do so, each selection includes apparatus that provides context for engaged reading and critical thinking. An informative headnote introduces the angle of inquiry that the reading explores and closes with Questions for a Closer Reading, which invite students to probe the selection's assumptions, evidence, and argument. At the end of the book, Making Connections questions offer students ways to read the essays against one another, showing how interesting problems emerge from the debate. Suggestions for Further Reading conclude each book, pointing interested students toward relevant materials for extended study.

Historical discourse is rarely a matter of simple opposition. These volumes show how ideas develop and how answers change, as minor themes turn into major considerations. The Historians at Work volumes bring together thoughtful statements in an ongoing conversation about topics that continue to engender debate, drawing students into the historical discussion with enough context and support to participate themselves. These books aim to show how serious scholars have made sense of the past and why what they do is both enjoyable and worthwhile.

EDWARD COUNTRYMAN

Preface

My colleague Edward Countryman provided the idea for this book when he suggested that I bring together several essays that examine the causes of the Pueblo Revolt of 1680, a dramatic event in the history of early America. In 1598, Spaniards came north from Mexico to plant a permanent colony in what is today New Mexico in the heart of the American Southwest. Eight decades later, Pueblo Indians destroyed the colony and drove Spaniards out of their lands. The conquered became the conquerors. That turn of events was so unusual that it continues not only to intrigue us but to demand explanation.

Like many other pivotal events, the Pueblo Revolt can be understood in a variety of ways, some of them mutually exclusive. It can be argued, for example, that the Pueblos foolishly and ungratefully rejected the blessings of Christianity and the advantages of European culture. Or a case can be made that by revolting, the Pueblos gained religious and economic freedom. The "facts" can sustain either argument, so how can we tell which is correct?

If we call on history to provide an answer, history will not reply with clarity. As with other moments in time, the Pueblo Revolt is gone. It lives on only in oral traditions, in the written words of those who witnessed it, and in the work of scholars who try to reconstruct it. None of these sources, however, can fully recapture the thoughts, conversations, and actions that led the Pueblos to revolt, much less give us a complete replay of the sequence of events. Witnesses of the revolt, be they Pueblos or Spaniards, were not everywhere at once, nor were they disinterested observers. Modern-day scholars, who have access to a greater range of sources than did any single person who lived through the revolt, do not have *all* the sources—least of all from the Indians. Moreover, scholars' selections and interpretations of the sources on the Pueblo Revolt (like other past events) are influenced by their own time, place, and sensibility, as the readings in this book make clear.

Why, then, do scholars bother to write about the Pueblo Revolt and why should we read their work? One answer is clear. We are curious about the past and how it shaped the present. In the United States, few places excite our curiosity more than New Mexico. A mecca for tourists who have long found it an exotic corner of America, today's New Mexico cannot be understood without reference to its early years. The most populous Spanish colony in what is now the United States, New Mexico stood deep in Indian country, amidst Pueblos, Navajos, Apaches, and other native tribes and bands. A moment of armed conflict like the Pueblo Revolt produced a flurry of writing that yields unusual insights into the relationships among these peoples, both before the conflict began and after it ended.

Historians know they cannot perfectly reconstruct past events like the Pueblo Revolt, but they try nonetheless to explain them to the best of their abilities. However imperfect, historians' ablest explanations of the past are rich, deep, and credible. They deserve to be read as important counterweights to the shrill simplifications of purveyors of popular culture or the incredible invocations of the past that come from the mouths and pens of demagogues and ideologues. Without careful reconstructions of the past, for example, we would be vulnerable to mythmakers who demonize all Indians or those who categorically ennoble them, and we would have no argument to offer against those who caricature Spaniards as villains or heroes.

These abstractions about the uses and limits of history can be easily stated. They cannot be fully appreciated and understood, however, except by reading historians themselves and comparing the answers they give to the same question or comparing the questions they raise about the same issue. Edward Countryman's Historians at Work series makes it easy for students to compare the work of historians, to raise their own questions, and provide their own answers. Happily, Countryman's selection of significant topics for this series also assures us that as students think about the American past they will meet all the peoples who make up the present-day United States, including Spaniards and Pueblos, whose interactions with one another preceded Jamestown and Plymouth.

Acknowledgments

I appreciate the kindness of Bedford/St. Martin's acquisitions editor Katherine Kurzman and Bedford/St. Martin's author and SMU colleague Ross Murfin, who, at a critical juncture, made it possible for me to do this book. I am also grateful to the writers who allowed me to reproduce their work in this volume and to several specialists who read an early version of the manuscript, saved me from errors, and pointed me in new directions: Colin Calloway from Dartmouth College, Harry A. Kersey from Florida Atlantic University, Jill Lepore from Boston University, Sherry L. Smith from the University of Texas, El Paso, and Mel Yazawa from the University of New Mexico. Bedford/St. Martin's Jen Lesar was a model editor.

DAVID J. WEBER

A Note for Students

Every piece of written history starts when somebody becomes curious and asks questions. The very first problem is who, or what, to study. A historian might ask an old question yet again, after deciding that existing answers are not good enough. But brand-new questions can emerge about old, familiar topics, particularly in light of new findings or directions in research, such as the rise of women's history in the late 1970s.

In one sense history is all that happened in the past. In another it is the universe of potential evidence that the past has bequeathed. But written history does not exist until a historian collects and probes that evidence (*research*), makes sense of it (*interpretation*), and shows to others what he or she has seen so that they can see it too (*writing*). Good history begins with respecting people's complexity, not with any kind of preordained certainty. It might well mean using modern techniques that were unknown at the time, such as Freudian psychology or statistical assessment by computer. But good historians always approach the past on its own terms, taking careful stock of the period's cultural norms and people's assumptions or expectations, no matter how different from contemporary attitudes. Even a few decades can offer a surprisingly large gap to bridge, as each generation discovers when it evaluates the accomplishments of those who have come before.

To write history well requires three qualities. One is the courage to try to understand people whom we never can meet — unless our subject is very recent — and to explain events that no one can re-create. The second quality is the humility to realize that we can never entirely appreciate either the people or the events under study. However much evidence is compiled and however smart the questions posed, the past remains too large to contain. It will always continue to surprise.

The third quality historians need is the curiosity that turns sterile facts into clues about a world that once was just as alive, passionate, frightening, and exciting as our own, yet in different ways. Today we know how past events "turned out." But the people taking part had no such knowledge. Good history recaptures those people's fears, hopes, frustrations, failures, and achievements; it tells about people who faced the predicaments and choices that still confront us as we head into the twenty-first century.

All the essays collected in this volume bear on a single, shared problem that the authors agree is important, however differently they may choose to respond to it. On its own, each essay reveals a fine mind coming to grips with a worthwhile question. Taken together, the essays give a sense of just how complex the human situation can be. That point — that human situations are complex — applies just as much to life today as to the lives led in the past. History has no absolute "lessons" to teach; it follows no invariable "laws." But knowing about another time might be of some help as we struggle to live within our own.

EDWARD COUNTRYMAN

Contents

"Instead of beginning with a belief that the natural world was
the Lord's footstool and man's economic resource, Indians of
the Rio Grande gave the earth a sacred status of its own."

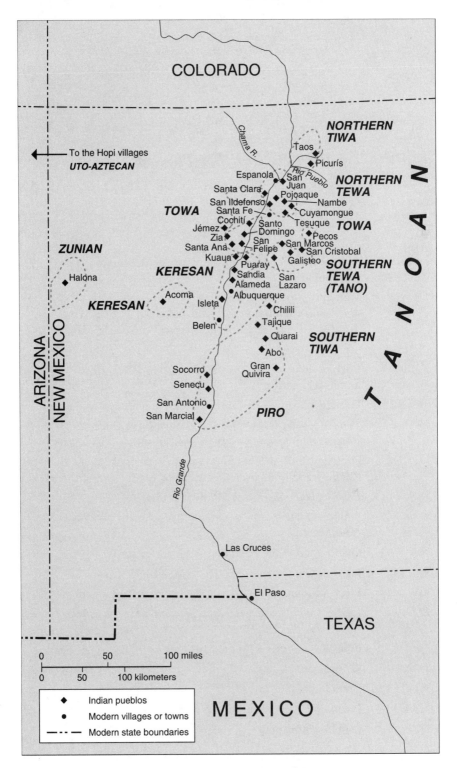

The Pueblos in the Sixteenth Century and Their Language Groups

Spaniards and Pueblos in New Mexico

A Chronology

ca. 800 B.C. to A.D. 400	Agriculture becomes important among distant ancestors of the Pueblos.
ca. A.D. 500	West and north of the Rio Grande, some of the Pueblos' ancestors develop the high culture known as Anasazi.
ca. 1000 to 1300	Anasazi culture reaches its zenith.
ca. 1300 to 1540	Pueblos, heirs to Anasazi traditions, flourish on the Rio Grande and its tributaries.
1540–42	Francisco Vázquez de Coronado enters the Pueblo country.
1565	*Pedro Menéndez de Avilés founds St. Augustine, Florida, the first permanent European settlement in what is now the United States.*
1581	Fray Agustín Rodríguez and Captain Francisco Sánchez Chamuscado rediscover New Mexico.
1585	*English plant a short-lived settlement at Roanoke.*
1598	Juan de Oñate establishes an enduring Spanish colony in New Mexico.
1598	Oñate destroys the Pueblo of Acoma.
1601	Many of Oñate's colonists flee to Mexico.
1605	Viceroy Montesclaros orders New Mexico abandoned.
1607	*English found Jamestown, the first permanent English settlement in what is now the United States.*
1608	Philip III authorizes Franciscans to remain in New Mexico.
ca. 1610	Santa Fe established.
1680	Great Pueblo Revolt.
1692–94	Diego de Vargas reconquers New Mexico.
1696	Pueblos revolt again.

PART ONE

Introduction

Pueblos, Spaniards, and History

Pueblos, Spaniards, and History

Pueblos and Spaniards

In 1680, in a swift and bloody revolt, Pueblo Indians over-threw the Spaniards who had occupied their lands for more than eighty years. Since 1598, when Juan de Oñate brought a small group of colonists into the mesa and canyon country of northern New Mexico, Spain had asserted its sovereignty over the Pueblo peoples. Spanish officials had demanded that Pueblos pay tribute to the Spanish Crown by working for *encomenderos,* a small number of privileged Spaniards to whom Spanish officials entrusted the Pueblos and their labor. At the same time, Spanish priests established missions in the Pueblos' farming villages and demanded that the Indians abandon their religion in favor of Christianity. Pueblo Indians, who vastly outnumbered their Spanish overlords, tolerated this arrangement for several generations before rebelling. Why did they wait so long? Why did they rebel at all?

Spaniards had first come to New Mexico to find treasure. As early as 1540 Francisco Vázquez de Coronado led a quixotic *entrada* into the Pueblo country in search of seven cities of gold. In 1598, when Juan de Oñate set out with the king's permission to plant a proprietary colony on the Rio Grande, he hoped to repay his substantial investment by finding rich mines like the fabulous silver strike that his father, Cristóbal, had made at Zacatecas. Farming and ranching also drew Spaniards into the northern regions of New Spain, but the hope of quick and great wealth had motivated the earliest Spanish explorers and settlers — as was the case with their English contemporaries who founded Roanoke and Jamestown.

Juan de Oñate's failure to find riches almost doomed his colony. In 1605, two years before Englishmen founded Jamestown and three years before Frenchmen founded Quebec, the viceroy in Mexico City recommended that Spaniards withdraw from New Mexico. Isolation and distance from the nearest settlements in New Spain, as Mexico was then called, made New Mexico too expensive to sustain. Spain had more lucrative colonies in mineral-rich Peru and Mexico.

Franciscans intervened. They objected to the abandonment of New Mexico on the grounds that their missionary work had advanced so far that they could not turn back. In contrast to Englishmen, who declined to convert Indians into Christians until they had turned them into Englishmen, Spaniards tried to convert Indians and turn them into Spaniards simultaneously.[1] Indeed, the Spanish Crown made the conversion of Indians to Christianity central to its enterprises in the New World. Spain's very claim to its American empire rested on papal bulls of 1493 that required Spanish monarchs to instruct natives in the Catholic faith. Additional papal bulls of 1501 and 1508 gave the Crown authority over the Church in America (the *patronato real*, or royal patronage). These effectively united church and state in Spain and left no doubt of the Crown's responsibility for Indian souls, even in remote New Mexico.

To fulfill its religious responsibilities, the Crown turned to members of religious orders of celibate males such as the Franciscans, whose order was founded by Francis Bernardone in 1209 in Italy. Robed and sandaled Franciscans came to New Mexico with Juan de Oñate in 1598 and began to establish themselves in Pueblo communities. Drawing on long experience at manipulating Indians elsewhere in the Americas, they convinced Pueblos to build churches and living quarters for them, and they tried to replace the Pueblos' religion with their own.

The Pueblos, whose own cultural tradition went back at least to the time that Europeans believed the son of their god, Jesus Christ, walked on earth, seemed ideal subjects for conversion. Like Iberians, the Pueblos lived in towns, farmed nearby fields, and wore what Spaniards recognized as clothing. Although they were not a homogeneous people and spoke several discrete languages, Spaniards named these Indians "Pueblos" because they lived in permanent towns (*pueblos*) of stone or adobe, in contrast to the nomads and seminomads whose lands Spaniards traversed to reach New Mexico. For Franciscans, who insisted that Indians live like Spaniards and tried to congregate them into towns if they did not, the apartment-dwelling Pueblos seemed a godsend. Although Franciscans failed to plant missions among Apaches, Navajos, and other seminomads who surrounded the Pueblo country, they succeeded among the Pueblos.

Where Oñate failed to find treasure, then, the Franciscans found souls. They explained to the Crown that they could not abandon the thousands of Pueblos whom they had brought into the Christian fold through the ritual they called baptism. To abandon the Pueblos meant depriving them of the Church's sacraments and endangering their souls, the Franciscans said. The Crown would either have to persuade thousands of Pueblo converts to leave their multi-storied villages and move south to Chihuahua to be near missionaries or allow the missionaries to remain in New Mexico. In 1608, the

Crown chose the more practical alternative. It authorized the Franciscans to remain in New Mexico, their expenses to be paid by the royal treasury.

Like Spanish Florida, which also received a reprieve from the Crown in 1608, New Mexico changed from a proprietary colony, funded largely by Oñate, to a Crown colony funded by the royal treasury. New Mexico became a center for missionary activity, with Pueblo Indians as its chief asset. Friars depended on Pueblo labor to make their missions work; colonists, whose numbers may not have reached three thousand in the 1600s, depended on Pueblo labor to operate their farms, ranches, and other enterprises from the gathering of pine nuts to the tanning of hides. The two groups — colonists and clergy — vied with one another for control of the lives and labor of the dwindling Pueblo population, which fell from around sixty thousand in the early 1600s to some thirty thousand in the 1640s to seventeen thousand by 1680. European contagious diseases probably took their familiar toll on the Pueblos. So perhaps did intertribal warfare and Spanish exploitation, which the Crown seemed powerless to stop. In that remote frontier province, far from the eyes of watchful officials, even appointed governors commonly abused their power over Indians.[2]

Until 1680, Pueblos tolerated the outsiders. An agricultural people, rooted to fertile valleys in a high desert land of little rain, Pueblos had no other place to go. Some tried to rebel, but revolts remained isolated affairs easily quashed by Spaniards. The autonomous Pueblo towns, separated by several hundred miles and at least six different languages and countless dialects, had no central government to unify them. Moreover, Pueblos knew that rebellion invited hideous retaliations. How could Pueblos forget the burning of the Pueblo of Ácoma when it offered resistance in 1598 and the punishments meted out to the survivors by Spaniards with swords of steel? Treating Indian miscreants as brutally as they treated one another, Spaniards cut the right foot off every male Ácoman over twenty-five years of age.

Rewards as well as punishments probably encouraged Pueblos to cooperate with Spaniards. New draft animals, new crops, and new metal tools from Iberia enriched Pueblo material culture. Spanish warriors proved useful allies against historic enemies, and unarmed Spanish priests, so powerful that Spanish warriors obeyed them, offered spiritual power. Through the 1600s, several generations of Pueblos found reasons to accommodate to and benefit from their new Spanish overlords.

Then, in a few weeks in the late summer of 1680, Pueblos destroyed the Spanish colony of New Mexico. Coordinating their efforts as they had never done before, Pueblos launched a well-planned surprise attack. From the kiva at Taos, Pueblo messengers secretly carried calendars in the form of knotted cords to participating pueblos. Each knot marked a day until the Pueblos would take up arms. The last knot was to be untied on August 11, but the rebellion exploded a day early. Tipped off by sympathetic Pueblos, Spaniards had captured two of the rebel messengers on August 9. When leaders of the revolt learned that they had been betrayed, they moved the attack up a day. Despite the warning, the revolt caught Spaniards off guard. They could not imagine the magnitude of the planned assault. Scattered in isolated farms and ranches along the Rio Grande and its tributaries, Spaniards were easy prey for the rebels.

Spanish refugees swarmed into Santa Fe, the province's one Spanish town, and to Isleta Pueblo, one of the few native towns that apparently did not join the rebellion. Believing themselves the only survivors, the refugees at Isleta retreated southward toward El Paso on September 14, joined by some Isletans. Meanwhile, Governor Antonio de Otermín tried to defend Santa Fe against a Pueblo siege. Outnumbered, losing ground, and with his water supply cut by Pueblo rebels, Otermín finally decided to abandon the smoldering town. Pueblo rebels allowed the Spaniards to leave Santa Fe on September 21. Joined by some of the Pueblos who had remained loyal to them, they too fled down the Rio Grande, joining the other refugees at El Paso, three hundred miles from Santa Fe. Governor Otermín estimated that the Pueblos had killed more than four hundred of New Mexico's Hispanic residents, whose total numbers did not exceed three thousand.[3] The rebels desecrated the churches and killed twenty-one of the province's thirty-three Franciscans, in many cases humiliating, tormenting, and beating them before taking their lives.

A dozen years passed before the Spaniards regrouped and began to reconquer the Pueblos' adobe villages under the leadership of Diego de Vargas. In the twelve-year interval, the glue that held most of the Pueblos together during the revolt had dissolved, and Vargas skillfully took advantage of Pueblo disunity. By 1694 he had cajoled or conquered Pueblo towns into submission, one by one. But Pueblo fealty to Spain existed only on the surface. As Franciscans reestablished missions in the pueblos, a deep undercurrent of resistance exploded once again, in 1696. Better prepared and more cunning than Governor Otermín had been in 1680, Vargas and his Pueblo allies waged a six-month war of attrition against the rebels, finally subduing all but the Hopi Pueblos (in today's Arizona), which Spain never reconquered.

The Pueblo Revolt of 1680 was one of several coincidental wars Indians waged against Europeans along North American contact zones in the late 1600s. In the 1670s, Englishmen moving westward from their colonies along the Atlantic coast faced heightened Indian resistance in New England with King Philip's War, in Virginia with the Susquehanna War, and in South Carolina, where English slave traders from Charleston encouraged Indians to make war on one another and on their Spanish neighbors in Florida. Beginning in 1680, the Carolinians' Yamasee and Creek allies began to attack the Spanish missions of Florida, selling mission Indians into slavery. Within a generation they destroyed a chain of Spanish missions that ran across northern Florida and up the Georgia coast.

Meanwhile, in southwestern North America, the Pueblo Revolt represented only one episode in what historian Jack Forbes called "the Great Southwestern Revolt." Across the northern edges of the viceroyalty of New Spain, which administered the New Mexico colony, Indians as various as Janos, Sumas, Conchos, Tobosos, Julimes, and Pimas fled from Spanish control to ravage missions and settlements. An "epidemic" of Indian rebellions seemed to have swept across northern New Spain in the 1680s.[4]

Until recently students of colonial American history in the United States were more likely to learn about King Philip's War than about the Pueblos' rebellion. Led by the English-educated Wampanoag chief Metacom (whom the English dubbed King Philip), Wampanoags, Narragansetts, and other Algonquian peoples nearly matched the Pueblos' achievement of temporarily ridding themselves of their conquerors. Beginning in 1675, they destroyed English towns throughout the interior and came close to forcing the colonists to abandon New England entirely. But the tide turned against King Philip when the Iroquois, for their own reasons, attacked the Algonquians and inadvertently benefited the English colonists. By summer of 1676, what the English called King Philip's War had ended with heavy fatalities on both sides but with Englishmen vanquishing the Algonquians so thoroughly that one historian has suggested that King Philip's War might be more aptly called "the Second Puritan Conquest."[5]

King Philip's War and the Pueblo Revolt took place at about the same time, in territory that has become part of the United States. King Philip lost to Englishmen, whose history in America we in the United States have made our own. His struggle has been well remembered by American historians and publishers with their traditional orientation toward the Northeast. The Pueblos, in contrast, defeated Spaniards who eventually lost their colonies, from California to Florida. Anglocentric American historians showed little interest in those former Spanish colonies, much less in the Pueblo Revolt.

Historians and the Pueblo Revolt

In recent years, however, historical sensibilities have begun to change along with economic, political, and demographic shifts. Teachers and writers of high school and college textbooks have sought increasingly to tell the stories of all the peoples who make up present-day America. The Pueblos' exceptional victory is beginning to interest us as much as King Philip's melancholy defeat.[6]

Although scholars of American history have slighted Pueblos and Spaniards, historians who study southwestern America or Latin America have long regarded the Pueblo Revolt as an important event: one of the most successful uprisings against Europeans in the New World. The Pueblo Revolt pales next to the more enduring victory of the Araucanians, who maintained autonomy for two centuries after destroying seven substantial Spanish towns in south-central Chile in 1598–1603, but the Pueblos' achievement was significant and unusual. It marked one of the rare moments in more than three hundred years of colonial rule in the Americas that Spaniards suffered a thorough defeat by natives whom they had long subjected. Moreover, most scholars believe that the Pueblos' act of defiance assured them of a measure of freedom from future Spanish efforts to eradicate their culture.

Scholars who have studied the Pueblo Revolt, then, have seen it as unusual and pivotal, and they have sought to understand its causes and its consequences. Why, scholars have wondered, did Pueblos revolt after so many years of coexistence with Spaniards? Why did Pueblos revolt in 1680? Why not earlier? Why not later? Were they responding to long-standing grievances, or to more recent provocations? Or to both? How did they achieve sufficient unity to overcome the distances and language barriers that divided their autonomous towns? Who were their leaders? What was the role of mixed bloods — people of Indian and Spanish blood who occupied space between the Pueblo and Spanish worlds?

Explaining motives of other peoples in other times is always a perilous enterprise; indeed, we often find it difficult to sort out our own motives for actions we ourselves take. The task of explaining the motives of Pueblo rebels of the late seventeenth century, however, is further complicated by the fact that Pueblos left no written accounts. Pueblo oral traditions have not provided significant insights into the Pueblo Revolt. Either memories have dimmed, as Pueblo scholar Joe Sando has noted, or Pueblos continue to keep their memories to themselves.[7]

Of necessity, Indian and non-Indian scholars alike have had to rely on Spanish sources to understand relations between Spaniards and Pueblos in seventeenth-century New Mexico. The Spanish sources have two serious liabilities. First, Spaniards could not easily understand the nuances of societies radically different from their own, a problem that perplexes trained anthropologists who try to enter other cultures today. Second, few Spanish sources remain. Many of the documents vanished when Pueblos took control of Santa Fe, New Mexico's capital. The rebels hauled papers out of the government building and the church and burned them in the plaza. Fortunately for scholars, however, government officials and Franciscan priests had sent reports out of New Mexico in the decades before the Pueblo Revolt. Many of those reports, preserved in the archives of Mexico and Spain, shed light on relations between Spaniards and Indians in the decades prior to the revolt of 1680.

The major sources for understanding the events leading up to the Pueblo Revolt, however, come from the days and months immediately after it, when officials and priests scrambled to explain their stunning loss of an entire province. In search of answers, they interrogated Pueblo Indians, both those who remained friendly to them and rebels whom they captured or who later rejoined them. The Pueblos' answers provide our clearest testimony about the nature of Pueblos' relationships with Spaniards, even though we must listen to Pueblo voices through Spanish interlocutors and translators, articulated and understood in the context of a crisis.

All explanations of the causes of the Pueblo Revolt, then, draw on the same slender body of evidence. Curiously, the heart of that evidence — contemporary reports and the testimony of Spaniards and Indians alike — is available in print largely in English translation, removing us still further from the voices of both Spaniards and Indians.[8] Historians who write about the Pueblo Revolt must use the readily accessible English translations or else travel to archives in Spain and Mexico or to repositories that contain copies of documents from those archives to consult original documents. Constrained by time and money, historians have put their faith in translations, which by their very nature are an imperfect medium even at their best.[9]

The questions that scholars have asked of this flawed evidence and the various answers they have read into it reveal much about history and the making of history. If we define history as *what happened* in the past, scholars generally agree about the series of events that led up to the Pueblo Revolt. If, however, we think of history as *our understanding* of the past (the past, after all, has vanished and all we have left is our understanding), historians' explanations of the coming of the Pueblo Revolt reveal much about historians' own interests, methods, and imaginations.

Spanish survivors of the Pueblo Revolt offered the earliest explanations for its coming as they tried to learn the details of their own recent and bitter history. Incontrovertible evidence that the Pueblos destroyed churches and killed priests convinced Spaniards that the Pueblos had rejected Christianity, and they explained that rejection in metaphysical terms. Some Spaniards said the revolt was the work of the devil. Other Spaniards saw it as the work of their own god, who they supposed had punished them for their sins. There is no record that any of the survivors blamed themselves for provoking Pueblos to revolt. In Mexico City in 1693, the great seventeenth-century savant Carlos de Sigüenza y Góngora studied the official reports and put responsibility entirely on the Pueblos. "Perhaps it was the idle life of their pagan neighbors which inspired them," Sigüenza y Góngora wrote, "or, more likely, it was their inborn hatred of the Spaniards."[10]

Since the Enlightenment, scholars have placed little credence in "inborn" or innate hatreds, much less in satanic influences or divine retribution, but most modern students of the Pueblo Revolt have wondered why some Pueblos despised Spaniards enough to drive them away or kill them. Many have seen religion as the primary cause.

The Pueblo rebels' manifest hostility toward the Franciscans, their churches, and their sacraments in 1680 have prompted most historians to explain the Pueblo Revolt as a blow for religious freedom, a reaction against Franciscans' efforts to obliterate the Pueblo religion. One eighteenth-century historian of New Mexico made that point, although he expressed the idea in quite different terms than modern scholars might employ. Writing in 1778, a century after the revolt, the Franciscan scholar Silvestre Vélez de Escalante offered two reasons for the Pueblos' violent outburst: "First, the love which many of the old men retain for their ancient mode of life, for their idolatry," and "second, the vexations and bad treatment which they had suffered from some Spaniards in many pueblos, the persecution of those Indians who were taken to be wizards."[11] A century later, in the 1880s, Anglo-American historians of New Mexico had come to similar conclusions. "Religious feeling was a very strong element among the causes which led to the revolution," L. Bradford Prince wrote in 1883, "and a bitter hatred [of] the Christianity of the Spaniards was evinced in every act during the struggle." The Pueblo Revolt, Hubert Howe Bancroft noted in 1889, was "founded . . . largely, on religious grounds."[12]

In the last half of the twentieth century, historians have continued to see religion as a primary cause of the Pueblo Revolt, but they have looked more deeply into Pueblo religion and have come to new understandings of its significance in bringing on the conflict. Informed by anthropologists, some of whom have been Pueblo Indians (most notably Edward Dozier of Santa Clara Pueblo and Alfonso Ortiz of San Juan), historians now know that Pueblos regarded the proper observance of their traditional religious ceremonies as essential to their earthly as well as their spiritual well-being. The divisions that many of us in the Western world make today between our civic, economic, political, and religious lives would have seemed completely foreign to seventeenth-century Pueblos (and the same might be said for seventeenth-century Spaniards). For them, all life was of a piece. Spanish attempts to quash Pueblo religious practices, then, did not merely threaten Pueblo religion but threatened the Pueblos' very existence.

These insights into Pueblo religion inform the work of Henry Warner Bowden and Ramón A. Gutiérrez, from whose writings I have drawn the first two selections in this anthology. Both Bowden and Gutiérrez place the revolt's immediate causes in the 1670s, when severe drought, accompanied by famine, disease, and intensified Apache raids made life perilous for Pueblos. As the Pueblos' lives deteriorated, they grew disenchanted with the Franciscan missionaries whose god did not provide rain, cure disease, or discourage Apache raiders. Pueblos then turned with new fervor to their traditional religion and tried to revitalize it. Spaniards responded to this religious revival by suppressing Indian ceremonial practices more vigorously than ever. Thus, accommodation or coexistence with Spaniards became impossible for Pueblo religious leaders in the 1670s. Rebellion seemed the only way to gain freedom to pray openly to the *katsinas,* the spirits of dead ancestors who brought rain and other blessings, and to revitalize the *kivas*—the round, windowless, subterranean structures in which Pueblo men had worshiped before the coming of Spaniards. For both Bowden and Gutiérrez, the Pueblos' quest for religious freedom was the primary cause of the Pueblo Revolt. In each of their accounts, the Pueblos repay Spanish iconoclasm in kind.

Both Bowden and Gutiérrez suggest that the bitterness that some Pueblo religious leaders harbored toward Franciscans smoldered beneath the surface long before the events of the 1670s. As one elderly Pueblo rebel, whom Gutiérrez cites, told Governor Otermín after the revolt:

> the resentment which all the Indians have in their hearts has been so strong, from the time this kingdom was discovered [by the Spaniards], because the religious [the Franciscans] and the Spaniards took away their idols and forbade their sorceries and idolatries . . . that he has heard this resentment spoken of since he was of an age to understand.[13]

Scholars have generally taken such statements at face value. They have accepted not only the view that religious strife was at the heart of the Pueblo Revolt but that Pueblos had long resented Spanish religious oppression and Spaniards' attempts to force them to live in the manner of Spanish Christians. Writing about 1940, historian France Scholes, whose archival research into New Mexico's seventeenth-century society has never been superseded, noted that "the Spanish conquest and occupation of [New Mexico] had been a major shock to native life and thought, and although the Indians made an outward adjustment to the new ways, they remained fundamentally loyal to their old culture tradition." The Spaniards, Scholes wrote, "apparently failed to understand that acceptance of European modes of life, especially a new faith, threatened the very foundations of Pueblo culture."[14] Similarly, Charles Wilson Hackett, who in 1942 edited two hefty volumes of translations of the principal documents pertaining to the Pueblo Revolt upon which scholars still depend, found the cause of the Pueblo Revolt in "the efforts of the Spaniards to suppress not only the religious beliefs but also the ancient habits and customs of the Indians."[15]

In contrast, historian Van Hastings Garner, whose essay "Seventeenth Century New Mexico" is the third selection in this book, argues that historians had emphasized "the religious character of the rebellion . . . far out of proportion to its actual relevance." The friars, he says, allowed Pueblos to continue their old religious practices at the same time that they adopted Catholic ceremonies and beliefs. Garner also challenges historians who had seen the Spanish exploitation of Indian labor, by Franciscans as well as government officials and *encomenderos,* as a fundamental cause of the Pueblo Revolt. As early as 1682, two years after the revolt, a royal attorney in Mexico City noted that Spaniards and Indians should live separately "since the many oppressions which they [the Pueblos] receive from the Spaniards have been the chief reason for the rebellion."[16] Early Anglo-American historians were more specific. They imagined that Spaniards drove Pueblos beyond the limits of their endurance by overworking them in mines in New Mexico — an argument weakened by the fact that mining scarcely existed in Spanish New Mexico.[17] In the twentieth century, historians have continued to see forced labor as a fundamental cause of the Pueblo Revolt, but they have looked at the abuses of the *encomenderos* rather than at fictitious mines.[18]

Garner acknowledges that Spaniards required Indians to work for them. He did not find that work so oppressive, however, that it provoked a violent response. Rather, he suggests, Indians benefited from Spanish technology, new crops, and improved ways to store crops as well as from Spanish military protection against Apache and Navajo raiders (both Athapascan-speaking peoples). In Garner's formulation, more harmony than disharmony characterized the Pueblo Indians' relations with New Mexico governors and colonists, who built a stable society based on "mutual needs." Spaniards brought prosperity to the Pueblos until drought, famine, and pestilence swept across the land in the 1670s. Garner, then, sees the essential causes of the Pueblo Revolt in immediate events: drought, famine, and Apache raids of the 1670s, the same events that Bowden and Gutiérrez see only as catalysts for a revolt caused by deeper religious and cultural differences.

Whether or not one accepts Garner's argument for all of the Pueblos, it goes far to explain why some of the Pueblos remained loyal to Spaniards even during and after the Pueblo Revolt. Like Algonquians, some of whom followed and some of whom opposed King Philip, Pueblos found their communities bitterly divided. During the revolt, historian John Kessell wrote, Pecos Pueblo split into "at least two factions, one of which chanted, 'Death to the Spaniards!,' and another which evidently did not."[19]

Scholars have offered reasons for the Pueblos' relatively stable relations with Spaniards prior to the 1670s as well as reasons for their rebellion. But how did the Pueblos achieve sufficient unity to rise up against the Spaniards on a single day? Spanish sources pointed to Popé of the Tewa-speaking pueblo of San Juan as the leader who coordinated the great revolt, and most historians have concurred. If they are right, then Popé himself might be seen as the principal cause of the revolt, for without his leadership it might not have happened, and Popé should take a place alongside Pontiac, Tecumseh, Crazy Horse, Chief Joseph, and other great Indian leaders. If his name does not come as readily to mind, it is probably because he fought against Spaniards rather than against the English speakers who have occupied the central place in the dominant narrative of our nation's history.[20]

Some scholars, however, do not see Popé's leadership as the cause of the Pueblo Revolt. The social unrest of the late 1670s, they argue, produced the leader; the leader did not produce the unrest. The revolt, Garner writes, "was neither the expression of nor dependent upon one sagacious Indian; rather, it was the consequence of the collapse of a long series of delicately balanced human relationships. . . . Popé was there to personify aboriginal frustration and antagonism." Here Garner points to a larger question about the relative importance of the individual in shaping large events — a question that continues to provoke debate among historians.

Nearly a decade before Garner questioned Popé's importance, Angélico Chávez, a Franciscan and a historian, offers a startling conjecture that Popé may not have been the key leader of the revolt at all. In a controversial article published in 1967 and reprinted here, Chávez argues that Pueblo Indians in general were not discontented with Spanish rule or with Catholicism (an argument Garner later echoed). Chávez places full responsibility for the Pueblo Revolt on religious leaders like Popé and then added a new twist: "Some of the principal and most intelligent . . . leaders" were mixed bloods and not pure Pueblo Indians. Precisely because they were mixed bloods, or *mestizos,* Chávez claims, they occupied key leadership positions in Pueblo society. First, they understood both the Pueblo and Hispanic worlds and thus were more effective leaders. Second, they harbored deep resentment toward pure-blooded Spaniards, who placed them on the lowest rung of the social ladder because of their mixed racial heritage. Living among the Pueblos, where they felt more at home, the *mestizo* leaders plotted against the Spanish elite.

Had he gone no further than explore the leadership roles of *mestizos,* Chávez's article would have been of interest. He went on, however, to argue that the brains behind the entire revolt was a mixed blood named Domingo Naranjo, basing his argument on an interpretation of genealogical evidence that no previous historian had considered. The idea, offered as a hypothesis, challenged conventional wisdom about the revolt's leadership. To accept Chávez's identification of Domingo Naranjo as the guiding force behind the Pueblo Revolt is, of course, to diminish the role of Popé. To accept the argument that a mixed blood rather than a pure-blooded Pueblo led the revolt raises questions about the Pueblos' ability to exert leadership or to coalesce around one of their own. Little wonder, then, that these arguments have sparked controversy — a controversy that reignited in 1997 when New Mexico politicians decided to place a statue of Popé in Washington, D.C., as one of the two notable citizens that each state is permitted to place in Statuary Hall.[21] Joe Sando, a historian from Jémez Pueblo who once embraced Chávez's argument, defends the state's choice of Popé by suggesting that Chávez had invented the role of Domingo Naranjo. He "made it up," Sando told a reporter in June 1997. "It's entirely wrong."[22]

Chávez's observations that seventeenth-century New Mexican society was not dichotomous, that mixed bloods occupied a large space between Spaniards and Pueblos, has echoed recently in Andrew Knaut's recent book-length study of the Pueblo Revolt. Knaut takes a different tack, suggesting that the distance between Spanish and Pueblo society lessened over the course of the seventeenth century, as Spaniards and Pueblos intermixed and as Spaniards adopted aspects of Pueblo culture and Pueblos adopted aspects of Spanish culture. Knaut sees these dual processes of racial mixture and acculturation as unsettling to the social order. *Mestizos,* who did not enjoy the full acceptance of pure-blooded Spaniards, had a "destabilizing effect" on the colony, he argues, because the blurring of cultural and racial lines undermined the Spaniards' political authority, which had been built on "domination through physical distance and cultural segregation."[23]

The essays in this book do not exhaust the different perspectives that historians and other scholars have brought to the Pueblo Revolt. The role of the Athapascans — Apaches and Navajos — in the revolt, for example, remains unclear. In the standard telling of the story, drought in the 1670s forced Athapascans to raid Pueblo settlements and intensified Pueblo antipathy toward Spaniards who failed to provide protection. Ethnohistorian John P. Wilson has questioned that line of thought. The causes of Apache raiding, he has argued, resulted more from the provocations of Spanish slave traders, who captured and sold Apaches to work in the mines of Chihuahua, than to drought. Apache raids, he suggested, were aimed not at Pueblos but at Spaniards. Spanish missionaries exaggerated the effect of Apache attacks in order to divert attention from the true causes of Pueblo discontent, the Pueblos' exploitation by Spaniards.[24] Wilson's argument helps explain why some Apaches conspired with Pueblos in the events of 1680, a story that historian Jack Forbes has also explored.[25]

The roles of Pueblo women also need clarification, and historians Cheryl

J. Foote and Sandra K. Schackel have moved the conversation in this direction. They argue that the sexual exploitation of Indian women by Spaniards — civil officials and missionaries alike — contributed to the tensions between the two societies in the years before the revolt. At the same time, they find that Pueblo men who led the rebellion used their own women "as sexual pawns," promising their followers an Indian woman for every Spaniard they killed.[26]

Finally, some historians think the Pueblo Revolt a turning point in Spanish-Pueblo relations. Rather than continue to risk the Pueblos' wrath, Spaniards in eighteenth-century New Mexico appear to have demonstrated greater tolerance for Pueblo religious practices and made fewer demands on Pueblo labor than before the revolt. As tensions between Spaniards and Pueblos abated in the eighteenth century, more Pueblos joined forces with Spaniards to fight against other Indians, including Navajos, Comanches, and Apaches. As Pueblos and Spaniards cooperated against common enemies, tensions between them eased still further. By rebelling, then, the Pueblos had not won permanent independence, but they won a degree of freedom. They had, in the words of Alfonso Ortiz, taught Spaniards to "live and let live . . . and even become friends and religious kinsmen [of the Pueblos], *compadres* and *comadres.*"[27]

This idea that the Pueblo Revolt represented a turning point in Spanish-Pueblo relations has also been reconsidered. Writing in the late 1980s, John Kessell agreed with the conventional wisdom that the nature of Spanish and Indian relations changed between the seventeenth and eighteenth centuries, but he did not see that shift as a simple legacy of the Pueblo Revolt or a response to a common enemy. Rather, he suggested that Diego de Vargas, who began the slow reconquest of New Mexico in 1692, was the primary instrument of change. In reconquering New Mexico after the Pueblo Revolt, Kessell argued, Vargas skillfully took advantage of Pueblo factionalism to win Pueblos to his side.[28] Vargas forged military alliances with Pueblos and served as godfather to baptized Pueblo children. In so doing Vargas established a pattern of accommodation for eighteenth-century New Mexico. Kessell also pointed to larger forces that might have brought about a shift in Spanish-Pueblo relations, including demographic change and new imperial priorities, but he saw Vargas and not the Pueblo Revolt as the turning point. When Kessell made this case in 1989 he was steeped in a large project to reproduce documents from the Vargas years in a multivolume series.[29]

In writing about the Great Pueblo Revolt, then, historians have studied a common body of evidence and agreed upon a common body of facts, yet they have produced strikingly different ways of explaining the causes and effects of that event. It could hardly be otherwise. Explaining causation is complicated, and evidence is slender. More important, as they mediate between past and present, historians bring different questions, knowledge, and sensibilities to their work, giving them different perspectives on the past. The cumulative effect of their efforts has been to give us a fuller and deeper picture of Spanish-Indian relations in a corner of the continent whose past is increasingly understood to form part of our nation's rich historical heritage.

Notes

1. For English priorities, see James Axtell, *The Invasion Within: The Contest of Cultures in Colonial North America* (New York: Oxford University Press, 1985), 131–33.

2. Estimates of the Pueblo population in 1600 vary wildly, so the extent of decline cannot be stated with certainty. Nor are causes entirely clear. See David J. Weber, *The Spanish Frontier in North America* (New Haven: Yale University Press, 1992), 407, n. 143, and the essays by Jonathan Haas and Winifred Creamer, "Demography of the Protohistoric Pueblos of the Northern Rio Grande, A.D. 1450–1680," and Albert H. Schroeder, "Protohistoric Pueblo Demographic Change," both in *Current Research on the Late Prehistory and Early History of New Mexico,* ed. Bradley J. Vierra and Clara Gualtieri (Albuquerque: New Mexico Archaeological Council, 1992), 21–28, 29–36.

3. Andrew L. Knaut, in *The Pueblo Revolt of 1680: Conquest and Resistance in Seventeenth-Century New Mexico* (Norman: University of Oklahoma Press, 1995), 133–34, recently disputed these conventional estimates. He suggests a lower Spanish population in New Mexico — a thousand or so — but he comes to this conclusion by defining Indians racially rather than culturally. Many of the "Mexican Indians" who lived among Spaniards had become culturally Spanish and seem likely to have identified more with Spaniards than with Pueblos.

4. The "epidemic" metaphor appears in the report of a military junta of July 9, 1684, quoted in Jack D. Forbes, *Apache, Navaho, and Spaniard* (1960; reprint, Norman: University of Oklahoma Press, 1994), 202.

5. Francis Jennings, *The Invasion of America: Indians, Colonialism, and the Cant of Conquest* (Chapel Hill: University of North Carolina Press, 1975), 298. Jill Lepore, in *The Name of War: King Philip's War and the Origins of American Identity* (New York: Knopf, 1997), explores the larger meaning of the war.

6. See, for example, the difference in coverage between Robert A. Divine et al., *America Past and Present* (Glenview, Ill.: Scott, Foresman, 1984), 84 (which does not even identify the Indians responsible for "a major uprising in 1680"), and John Mack Faragher et al., *Out of Many: A History of the American People* (Engelwood Cliffs, N.J.: Prentice Hall, 1994), 51–53, which treats the Pueblo Revolt at length.

7. Joe S. Sando, "The Pueblo Revolt," *Handbook of American Indians,* vol. 9, *Southwest,* ed. Alfonso Ortiz (Washington, D.C.: Smithsonian Institution, 1979), 194–97, a historian from Jémez Pueblo, notes that his account utilizes "Pueblo oral tradition," but his essay is informed overwhelmingly by Spanish sources. A decade later, Sando lamented to John Kessell that so little remained in Pueblo oral tradition. John L. Kessell, "Spaniards and Pueblos: From Crusading Intolerance to Pragmatic Accommodation," *Columbian Consequences,* vol. 1, *Archaeological and Historical Perspectives on the Spanish Borderlands West,* ed. David Hurst Thomas, 3 vols. (Washington, D.C.: Smithsonian Institution Press, 1989), 135.

8. Some documents have been published in Spanish, but most exist in print only in Charles Wilson Hackett, ed., *Revolt of the Pueblo Indians of New Mexico and Otermín's Attempted Reconquest, 1680–1682,* trans. Charmion Clair Shelby, 2 vols. (Albuquerque: University of New Mexico Press, 1942). Native American historians remain insistent, nonetheless, that scholars consult living Indians about the distant past. See, for example, Susan A. Miller's and Theodore S. Jojola's essays in Devon Mihesuah, ed., *Natives and Academics: Researching and Writing about American Indians* (Lincoln: University of Nebraska Press, 1998), 103–04; 177.

9. See, for example, notes to the selection from the work of Ramón Gutiérrez in this book and the notes to Knaut, *Pueblo Revolt.* For the dangers of relying on translations, see Jerry R. Craddock, "Juan de Oñate in Quivira," *Journal of the Southwest* (forthcoming).

10. Irving Albert Leonard, ed. and trans., *The Mercurio Volante of Don Carlos de Sigüenza y Góngora: An Account of the First Expedition of Don Diego de Vargas into New Mexico in 1692* (Los Angeles: Quivira Society, 1932), 55.

11. Silvestre Vélez de Escalante, *Letter of the Father Fray Silvestre Vélez de Escalante Written on the 2d of April, in the Year 1778: The Earliest History of California, New Mexico . . .* (Ramona, Calif.: Acoma Books, 1983), 6.

12. L. Bradford Prince, *Historical Sketches of New Mexico* (Kansas City: Leggat Brothers, 1883), 193, 196, and Hubert Howe Bancroft, *History of Arizona and New Mexico, 1530–1888* (1889; facsimile reprint, Albuquerque: Horn and Wallace, 1962), 174. Henry Warner Bowden, in "Spanish Missions, Cultural Conflict, and the Pueblo Revolt of 1680," *Church History* 44 (June 1975): 226, argues that "none of the standard interpretations of Spanish activity and Pueblo resistance in the seventeenth century have noticed the important role religion played in the tensions between the two cultures." He cites Bancroft and Ralph Emerson Twitchell, *The Leading Facts of New Mexican History,* 2 vols. (1911–12; facsimile reprint, Albuquerque: Horn and Wallace, 1963), 1:354–55, but Twitchell quotes Bancroft at length, in apparent approval. Bowden also cites Charles Wilson Hackett as one who overlooked the religious cause, but that is not the case. See Hackett, *Revolt of the Pueblo Indians,* 1:xxii. See also Forbes, *Apache, Navaho, and Spaniard,* 178.

13. Declaration of Pedro Nanboa of the pueblo of Alameda, in Hackett, *Revolt of the Pueblo Indians,* 1:61.

14. France V. Scholes, *Troublous Times in New Mexico, 1659–1670,* Historical Society of New Mexico, Publications in History, vol. 11 (Albuquerque: University of New Mexico Press, 1942), 257. This work first appeared serially in the *New Mexico Historical Review* in 1940–41.

15. Hackett, *Revolt of the Pueblo Indians,* 1:xxii.

16. Martín de Solís Miranda, Mexico, June 24, 1682, quoted in Hackett, *Revolt of the Pueblo Indians,* 2:402.

17. Josiah Gregg, *Commerce of the Prairies,* ed. Max L. Moorhead (1844; reprint, Norman: University of Oklahoma Press, 1954), 86; Prince, *Historical Sketches,* 190–91.

18. See, for example, the Pueblo anthropologist Edward P. Dozier, *The Pueblo Indians of North America* (New York: Holt, Rinehart, and Winston, 1970), 71, and H. Allen Anderson, "The Encomienda in New Mexico, 1598–1680," *New Mexico Historical Review* 60 (October 1985), 372, who ignores religious causes.

19. John L. Kessell, *Kiva, Cross, and Crown: The Pecos Indians and New Mexico* (Washington, D.C.: National Park Service, 1979), 232. Elizabeth A. H. John, in *Storms Brewed in Other Men's Worlds: The Confrontation of Indians, Spanish, and French in the*

Southwest, 1540–1795 (College Station: Texas A&M University Press, 1975), 99–100, offers several reasons why some Pueblos retained close ties with Spaniards or resisted following the rebel leadership.

20. Popé does merit a chapter in Alvin M. Josephy Jr., *The Patriot Chiefs: A Chronicle of American Indian Leadership* (New York: Viking Press, 1961), 63–96.

21. In 1997, the New Mexico legislature passed, and the governor signed, such a bill. Since 1864, each state has had the right to place two statues of notable citizens in Statuary Hall in the U.S. Capitol. New Mexico, which became a state in 1912, made its first selection in 1965, choosing U.S. Senator Dennis Chávez.

22. Quoted in Kate Nelson, "Popé, a Marauder or Freedom Fighter?" *Albuquerque Tribune,* June 5, 1967, B-3. For Sando's earlier acceptance of Chávez's argument, see Joe S. Sando, *The Pueblo Indians* (San Francisco: Indian Historian Press, 1976), 57, and Sando, "Pueblo Revolt," 195.

23. Knaut, *Pueblo Revolt,* 140, 150–51.

24. John P. Wilson, "Before the Pueblo Revolt: Population Trends, Apache Relations, and Pueblo Abandonments in Seventeenth-Century New Mexico," *Prehistory and History in the Southwest: Collected Papers in Honor of Alden C. Hayes,* Papers of the Archaeological Society of New Mexico, no. 11, ed. Nancy L. Fox (Albuquerque: Archaeological Society of New Mexico, 1985), 113–20.

25. Forbes, *Apache, Navaho, and Spaniard.*

26. Cheryl J. Foote and Sandra K. Schackel, "Indian Women of New Mexico, 1535–1680," *New Mexico Women: Intercultural Perspectives,* Joan M. Jensen and Darlis A. Miller (Albuquerque: University of New Mexico Press, 1986), 29.

27. Alfonso Ortiz, "Popay's Leadership: A Pueblo Perspective," *El Palacio* 86 (Winter 1980–Winter 1981): 22.

28. Kessell, "Spaniards and Pueblos," 127–38.

29. John L. Kessell, ed., *Remote Beyond Compare: Letters of don Diego de Vargas to His Family from New Spain and New Mexico, 1675–1706* (Albuquerque: University of New Mexico Press, 1989), was the first of those volumes.

PART TWO

Some Current Questions

The selections that follow deal with some of the issues about the Pueblo revolt that now interest historians. Other questions and other selections could have been chosen, but these show the current state of the conversation. Each selection is preceded by a headnote that introduces both its specific subject and its author. After the headnote come Questions for a Closer Reading. The headnote and the questions offer signposts that will allow you to understand more readily what the author is saying. The selections are uncut and they include the original notes. The notes are also signposts for further exploration. If an issue that the author raises intrigues you, use the notes to follow it up. At the end of all the selections are more questions, under the heading Making Connections. Turn to these after you have read the selections, and use them to bring the whole discussion together. In order to answer them, you may find that you need to reread. But no historical source yields up all that is within it to a person content to read it just once.

1. Did Pueblos revolt to save their traditions?

Henry Warner Bowden

Spanish Missions, Cultural Conflict, and the Pueblo Revolt of 1680

In the following article, first published in 1975, Henry Bowden sees religion as the heart of both Spanish and Pueblo cultures and the primary cause of the Pueblo Revolt. Bowden errs in this article when he asserts that "none of the standard interpretations . . . have noticed the important role religion played in the tensions between the two cultures." To the contrary, standard interpretations stress religious differences, as the introduction to this book makes clear (see, too, note 12 of the introduction). Although Bowden's argument is not as novel as he suggests it is, he advances it in a fresh way, giving us the most penetrating examination to date of the relationship between Spanish Catholicism and Pueblo religion.

In contrast to earlier writers, Bowden finds striking similarities between Pueblo religion and Spanish Catholicism and so helps us understand why Pueblos tolerated Spanish missionaries, at least initially. He also explains the deep incompatibility of the two religious systems, thus making the Pueblo Revolt more understandable. Although he recognizes that Pueblos revolted for many reasons, he argues that religion was the root cause.

Bowden bases his analysis on the familiar historical sources that earlier historians utilized, but he brings to them insights from anthropology and the history of religion, and he uses comparisons between Pueblo religion and Christianity as devices to better explain the nature of each religion.

Trained in the history of religion at Princeton, Henry Bowden has spent a long career as professor of religion at Rutgers University, New Brunswick, New Jersey. The article that follows was first published in 1975 in the scholarly journal *Church History;* a modified version appears as a chapter in Bowden's book *American Indians and Christian Missions: Studies in Cultural Conflict* (Chicago: University of Chicago Press, 1981), in which he compares the interactions among Indians and French, English, and American missionaries. In all cases, he found, missionaries had adverse effects on Indian cultures, their lofty motives notwithstanding.

Bowden's use of "red men" in the article reveals that he was writing in another era, but his shrewd opening comments about the pitfalls and possibilities of understanding other cultures in other times could have been written today.

Questions for a Closer Reading

1. In what ways does Bowden find Spanish Catholicism and Pueblo religious beliefs compatible?

2. In what ways does he find them incompatible?

3. Why didn't Franciscans understand the nature of Pueblo religion, according to Bowden?

4. What, according to Bowden, has anthropology revealed about Pueblo religion that Spaniards of the 1600s did not understand?

5. Why does Bowden argue that Pueblos' religious beliefs were more important than Apache raids or drought in causing them to revolt in 1680?

Spanish Missions, Cultural Conflict, and the Pueblo Revolt of 1680

Historians who try to understand encounters between red men and white men in the seventeenth century are immediately confronted with a problem: Indians were not literate, and they left no records of the sort we are accustomed to studying. For centuries, the only information about aboriginal populations in the Americas was derived from European narratives, conditioned by viewpoints that harbored an outsider's values. Archaeology added some indigenous references, but the evidence has usually been too meager for adequate generalization. Historians have pursued the goal of avoiding white men's biases and viewing Indian cultures as having an integrity all their own, but that goal has remained an ideal, causing more despair than hope of eventual success. As far as the history of early New Mexico is concerned, the situation is worsened by the fact that most church and government archives were burned during the fighting of 1680–1696.

In the twentieth century contributions of anthropological field workers have provided a wealth of new learning about Indian life. This scientific information is less distorted by culturally conditioned biases, and its disclosures are not tied to European source materials. Our modern data afford independent perspectives, new sources of information and opportunities for revising historical knowledge. A discriminating use of anthropological materials can free us from the narrow vision of a single cultural viewpoint and allow us more adequately to interpret past events that involved separate cultural units. Students of history now have the opportunity to work with new tools and ask new questions in addition to applying familiar methods to fresh data.

From an anthropologist's perspective, we can utilize a more comprehensive definition of religion and study its functional qualities in a particular cultural setting.[1] That kind of inquiry makes it possible to understand the

Henry Warner Bowden, "Spanish Missions, Cultural Conflict, and the Pueblo Revolt of 1680," *Church History* (1975): 217–28.

content of any people's world view, the unifying and normative place which religion has in the society's ethos and, most important, those aspects posing fundamental contrasts to alien cultures. The selection of Spanish missionary efforts in seventeenth-century New Mexico may be especially fruitful for a new interpretation of certain historical events because it provides a context in which the religious focus was apparent and significant for both cultures. The Rio Grande Pueblos organized most of their activities around a well-articulated system of religious symbols and practices; the Spaniards had long been conscious of religious motives behind many of their heroic efforts. An analysis of what was really at issue between Spanish and Pueblo cultures on the religious level can shed light on their similarities, antipathies and reasons for armed conflict between them.

Of course anthropological information is not a panacea to be used uncritically, and one must confront the difficulties involved in a study that proceeds from present observations back into the past. It may be that contemporary reports of Pueblo rituals, calendar cycles, social structure and so forth, represent patterns that did not exist in the same configurations during the 1600s.[2] It is also possible that an analysis of conflicts between the religions of Indian and Spaniard could highlight tensions disproportionately. Points of conflict in a specific context will indicate what was cherished enough at that time to defend against external pressures for change. But such conflicts do not show us the relative value of those cultural elements in a setting where they were unchallenged and allowed to seek their own level. The best we can hope for in studying two cultures is to identify their salient features in the limited context of their confronting each other. One should not conclude from comparative study that the controverted issues were categories of major significance within a society, relative to their own hierarchies of values.[3] Another pitfall to avoid is that of attributing awareness or deliberate motives to people when they may not have been conscious of the issues in the way we describe them. Historical events must be interpreted with ideas based on as much information as relevant sources provide, but we can never go on to say that those specific categories and definitions were in the minds of the protagonists at the time.[4] Despite these difficulties, it is still fair to say that facts and insights from anthropologists provide new avenues in the historian's search for an adequate understanding of red-white contact and the role religions played in the process. What follows is an attempt to demonstrate the results of such a study conducted within a limited area.

In 1598 the upper Rio Grande valley was viewed as an outpost of Spanish civilization, an opportunity for colonizing, mining and missionary exploits. By that time it had been the home of Keresan- and Tanoan-speaking Indians for over three hundred years. Under the leadership of Juan de Oñate an initial force of 400 persons, including 10 Franciscan friars, made their way upriver to the territory where approximately 30 to 40 thousand Pueblos inhabited an estimated 75 to 80 permanent towns. The first decade was a time of mismanagement and unsteady beginnings for both churchmen and civilians, but in 1609 the crown stabilized the colony with strong financial and administrative support, largely for the sake of its missionary enterprise.[5] With Santo Domingo and Santa Fe established as bases of operations for church and state respectively, the prospects for growth were bright.

Missionary work among the Indians seemed to go well from the outset. As village leaders of the six tribal groups became acquainted with the friars and their message, they are reported to have welcomed them, expressed polite interest in their ideas and asked to know more.[6] The district was soon divided into mission stations, and though the manpower shortage spread them thinly, priests were assigned to cover each area. Congregations were formed; catechetical instruction was begun; slowly a number of churches and chapels were built adjacent to the major pueblos. Various statistical reports of this period are not very reliable, but a realistic estimation is that an average of less than thirty Franciscans labored among colonists and natives during the seventeenth century and ministered to a baptized population of approximately 20,000 Pueblos.[7]

One cannot discern a pattern of constantly increasing growth. There was a great deal of internescine strife between ecclesiastical and governmental authorities, and missionary efforts seem to have been hampered as a result.[8] By 1630 the missions had spread numerically and geographically as far as they could in view of their problems with secular opposition, replacement difficulties and delays in supply and communication.[9] After that, their history is one of trying to maintain the level of achievement rather than pursuing larger and more ambitious objectives.

Converting more people to Christian practices was, nevertheless, the reason for New Mexico's existence, and the friars performed their tasks with singleness of purpose. That zeal led them to concentrate on restricting Indian religious activities, especially during the 1670s. There had been some conflict between native and Spanish priests from the start,[10] and sporadic outbursts of hostility had occurred at intervals,[11] but in 1675 the clash of cultures became more pronounced on each side with resentment and bitterness increasing proportionately. Native ceremonies and liturgical articles had long been outlawed by Spanish officials, but those injunctions were suddenly enforced with renewed vigor. Essential ceremonial chambers (*kivas*) and many altars were seized, dances were strictly forbidden, masks and prayer sticks were destroyed, priests and medicinemen were imprisoned, flogged or hanged.[12] Throughout the decade there was a determined action by both arms of Spanish culture to eradicate every vestige of Indian life, world view as well as ethos.

In August 1680 a general uprising of native peoples put a stop to those repressive measures. Every pueblo from Acoma to Pecos, from Taos to Isleta rose to destroy the Spanish presence north of El Paso. Of the 2,500 colonists approximately 380 were killed, including 21 of the 33 resident friars. All survivors were forced to retreat south, taking what few possessions they could carry while fleeing for safety.[13] The successful Indians methodically rid themselves of every reminder of Spanish intrusion. They destroyed a great deal of property, including churches with their records, images and ceremonial paraphernalia. Renouncing the alien faith, Pueblos bathed to cleanse themselves from the effects of baptism. They abandoned foreign dress, stopped using Spanish names and left their Christian wives. Their rejection of Hispanic cultural patterns and the restoration of revitalized native ways was as thorough as the united efforts of chiefs and people could make them.[14]

Why did the revolt occur? What were the primary factors leading to bloodshed at that particular time, and what can account for its deliberately anti-ecclesiastical character? Ranches and government buildings were also hit, but almost every church in the territory was demolished. Colonists of all types were killed when unfortunate enough to be caught in vulnerable positions, but the clergy were usually the first to die in every pueblo. Why did the spokesmen and symbols of Christianity receive the concentrated fury of Pueblo vengeance? The answer to these questions can be sought in a study of religions, their nature and place in the two cultures whose conflict rose to such an overt level. Religion was a factor at the core of each way of life, and if we can understand what contrasted at the center, we will be in a better position to interpret conflicts in the wider circles of cultural interaction, even to the point of seeing reasons for war.

During the initial stages of red-white contact there were enough similarities between their religions to allow for a degree of mutual understanding. On the tangible level, each side used altars, religious calendars, aids for prayer (feathered sticks or rosary beads), luxurious costumes for a distinct priesthood which presided over regularly appointed ceremonies, ritual chants in languages somewhat removed from everyday usage. Christian baptism corresponded easily to the Pueblo practice of head washing and the giving of a new name when one was initiated into special organizations. Catholic saints elevated from the ranks of men and women formed a parallel with Pueblo heroes who once lived among the people in human shape, now petitioned as powerful spirits. Spaniards were wont to experience visions, demonic as well as beatific, and this too provided a link with a people who saw horned snakes, cloud people (*shiwanna*) and witches. The use of incense and holy water was close to Pueblo priests who made "clouds" with yucca suds for rain or sprayed consecrated water on an ailing patient. Kissing the hand of a friar was likened to the practice of "drawing in the breath" of a native priest or a loved one.[15]

More intangibly, each religious system was based on beliefs that the world was ordered according to divine sanctions. The wills and wisdom of dominions beyond human making were thought by adherents of both cultures to be actively engaged in directing the weather, fortunes of war, personal fate and national destiny.[16] Conversely both interpreted disease, drought and famine as either the result of malevolent spirits or the displeasure of gods who would not overlook human frailty. Within these positive and negative emphases it would be difficult to say whether the love of good or fear of evil predominated in the day-to-day actions of either people. But each religion in its own way emphasized divine power as that which gave order and meaning to their adherents' identity and mode of life.

These similarities were not appreciated by the Franciscans in New Mexico as an avenue for introducing their mission program. Unlike the Jesuits in Arizona and northwestern Mexico, they did not begin by utilizing aspects of existing religion and move from them to Christian formulations. Instead they were convinced either that the Indians possessed no religion at all or that they had been lured by the Devil into a repugnant congeries of idol worship and superstition. These spiritual conquerors matched their military counterparts in holding that the natives were barbarians who lacked any civilized notion of law or legitimate authority.[17] Indian settlements were not viewed as properly organized communities; their forms of body covering were not considered true clothing; their sexual practices were judged to be disgracefully unregulated. So from the outset the friars set themselves the goal of stamping out every particle of native religion and substituting Catholic doctrines and practices, using force if necessary.

In keeping with these attitudes the Franciscans' behavior toward the Pueblos' religion conflicted sharply with tangible aspects of local custom. Almost without exception they did not try to master native languages or translate Christian ideas into them. They insisted that Indians learn Spanish. To supplant misguided native beliefs and ceremonial patterns, the missionaries operated on a policy of compulsory attendance at mass — for all baptized Indians but not all Spaniards. They made native officials (*fiscals*) punish their own people for failure to conform to this rule. With the aid of governors and soldiers they raided ancient ceremonial chambers and tried to prevent their future use. Masks and ritual paraphernalia of all kinds were periodically confiscated and burned. Traditional leaders who persisted in continuing the old rituals were arrested, and the gentle sons of St. Francis directed that they be whipped or executed as a menace to this life and an obstacle to the next.[18]

These areas of tension in physical confrontations were symptoms of more fundamental conflicts that lay beneath the surface. No one at that time seemed to realize how different their cultural orientations were, but modern anthropology has helped us see that there were serious contradictions between Pueblo and Spaniard in the categories of world view, personal identity and moral obligation.

Pueblo views of the world were diametrically opposed to western European ones. The underworld rather than heaven or the sky was their locus for sources of life. There was no reference to a primal god, an *ex nihilo* creation of matter, or any transcendental direction over the affairs of the natural world. Gods, men, animals and plants emerged through an opening in the underworld's roof (seen as a navel or *shipapu* from earth, the middle stratum of the cosmos), and all of them came from below to dwell on the surface of this world.[19] In the time of beginnings many gods or *katsina* had lived with the people and taught them how to cope with their new environment. Patterns and procedures thought to stem from that time and from those sources carried the sanction of ultimate authority:

> Thus the Indians got their culture — their houses, weapons, tools, and culti-
> vated plants, their clans, priests and societies, their songs, prayers, cere-
> monies and paraphernalia. That is why they live, work and worship . . . as they
> do: because their ways of life were established by the gods long ago. . . . To
> ignore or violate, to lose the customs of the old days . . . [would be] to bring
> misfortune . . . even extinction, upon themselves.[20]

Compared with the Spanish notion of a heavenly creator who guided his people from above, the Pueblo view derived strength from the opposite direction, and it was much more explicit about divinely instituted patterns of activity.

Instead of beginning with a belief that the natural world was the Lord's footstool and man's economic resource, Indians of the Rio Grande gave the earth a sacred status of its own. In comparison with Europeans who felt free to use natural materials for any secular purpose they fancied, Pueblos had a more profound respect for the basically sacred constitution of natural objects. Their place in this world was what really mattered to them, and sacred space radiated in concentric circles from the center, which was either the local village or a nearby place of emergence.[21] Everything in the cosmos had its place by reference to this center. Everything from points on the compass to changing seasons was bounded and controllable because the earth was an orderly environment that circumscribed the harmony of all good things.

Instead of wishing to escape this world or destroy it through exploitation, Pueblos affirmed their existence in it and husbanded their lives along with nature as parts of a single sanctified life system. It was a complete, substantial and satisfying world, and one could know enough about life, death and proper conduct to feel gratified by living in it according to established ways.[22]

Another point at which the two cultures stood in striking contrast to each other had to do with personal identity; that is, their worlds were different, and they thought of the people in them differently too. The European view enhanced the role of the individual, his free choice and opportunities to distinguish himself from others. Whether by valor or charity, by deeds of might or sacrifice, personal merit was a virtue to be prized and cultivated. For Pueblos, however, personal identity was always defined by reference to the community, not at its expense.[23] The self as any Spaniard would have defined it was submerged, and all of Indian society's values emphasized the well-being of the collectivity rather than that of the individual. Personal distinction was shunned, not sought; innovation was discouraged. Anyone who strove constantly to distinguish himself from his fellows was more likely to be ostracized and charged with witchcraft than to receive admiration from his townspeople.

The antithetical nature of this cultural trait is fairly easy to see when measured against Christian doctrines of salvation and the church. From its beginnings Christianity has almost always conveyed the assumption that its adherents were a separate people, sheep separated from the goats, wheat from the chaff, a faithful remnant saved from destruction by a merciful God. This salvation of separate individuals has usually included some degree of voluntary belief and personal morality, a combination of faith and works in which the responsibility of the believer played an important role in securing the final result. In Pueblo life there were no such thoughts. Everyone belonged to the group, and everyone was certain to reach the afterworld (enter *shipapu*), regardless of his merits or demerits. The only qualification on this cultural universalism was the idea that those failing to lead a good life would have a more difficult time reaching the place of emergence/reentry. There was no place of reward for the good and another of retribution for those less virtuous. As one valuable description put it, "to die in a pueblo is not to become dead but to return to the only real life there is; one 'changes houses' and rejoins the ancestors. . . ."[24] Just as there was no community-separating heaven and hell, there was no concept of atonement, no vicarious sacrifice, no redemption — none of these because there was no need.[25]

Christianity came to the Pueblos preaching doctrine that required a psychological sense of separation from the aboriginal group. The missionaries saw the church as an institution composed of believers gathered in an-ticipation of ultimate rescue out of this life. The church thus embodied a community-dividing thrust. Not all members of society would be saved, only the baptized. Not all Indians or Spaniards were expected at mass (and inci-dently punished for failure to attend), only those gathered into the com-munion of saints. The church cut through families and clans, through moities and secret societies.[26] Its contrast with native religious forms was stark enough when it stood simply as a competitive institution; but its major threat to native life stemmed from a disruptive capacity to offer salvation only to individuals.

Differing ideas of moral obligation comprised a third general category of conflict. For Spanish preachers ethical guidelines were thought to derive from biblical and theological traditions, sources transcending any particu-lar cultural group. Pueblos derived their sense of duty and propriety within an understanding of the community and its needs. The missionaries de-fined good and bad actions on a standard possessed by the church, seen as a divine institution that did not, in ideal terms at least, coincide with the to-tality of any cultural unit or their various civil offices. Natives based their model of ethical judgment on a standard that comprehended all facets of their society and did not see any reason for going beyond them. Europeans thought that sanctions against improper conduct would apply in the after-life, usually in addition to, not in place of, temporal effects. Indians ex-pected ultimate sanctions, like death for witchcraft, to apply in this life with no rewards or punishments reserved for the future.

The more important differences between Indian and European emerged in actually trying to live by these divergent views of right conduct while at-tempting to convert one's opposite number. The friars stressed attendance at mass, morning and evening prayer, monogamy with no divorce and obedience to Spanish magistrates as fundamental elements of moral life. Pueblo activities were aligned with the order of nature and had been orga-nized into an elaborate system of societies which presided over a cycle of rit-ual ceremonies. The Indians' central obligation was to participate in and to perpetuate those rites which insured a well-ordered life for the pueblo and its circle of physical needs.[27] Most village adults belonged to at least one of many societies, usually from eight to twenty in a pueblo, that presided over vital functions like planting, irrigation or rain making, hunting, harvesting, rules enforcement and curing physical ailments.[28] Existence itself, the very elements that gave meaning and structure to Indian life as a cultural unit, depended on cycles of corporate activity grouped rationally around an agrarian calendar year. Social structures conformed to the works necessary for cooperating with natural rhythms. Ritual activities were orchestrated to facilitate these works; food, shelter and health followed as a result of attention to ceremonial obligations.[29] If this combination of activities and moral obligations were ever suppressed to a serious degree, the threat to Pueblo existence would be quite serious indeed.

None of the standard interpretations of Spanish activity and Pueblo resistance in the seventeenth century have noticed the important role religion played in the tensions between the two cultures. They have usually stressed disputes over land and water rights, abuses in the *ecomienda* labor system or the obtrusive presence of a military *entrada* in another nation's territory. The major theme in historical writing for well over a century now has been to interpret Indian rebellion as an expression of economic and political self-determination. Discussions of the Pueblo Revolt of 1680 thus parallel other patriotic revolutions in the western hemisphere against a familiar archetype of tyranny and oppression.[30]

But is this an adequate explanation? It does not account for why the uprising occurred when it did, that is, why the various nations were desperate enough at that particular time to combine their strength and cooperate as never before. It does not explain why a war ostensibly over land, labor and personal freedom should have taken such an overtly anti-Christian turn. It implies that Spanish civil and ecclesiastical authorities would have been successful if their means had been less harsh. It fails to realize how antithetical the two cultures really were in the seventeenth century and how deeply the Pueblos were committed to maintaining the integrity of their cultural system, one that grounded their existence in realities they knew always to have pertained. Interpretations of the conflict offered thus far have overemphasized the political and economic factors, leaving several important questions unanswered and omitting consideration of relevant information about the values and motivations of people actually confronting a rival culture.

Suggestions for a more adequate historical interpretation would build on the physical and non-material cultural differences already discussed and then concentrate on events beginning in 1667. From that year to 1672 there was an extended drought and crop failure. Most of the population, Indian and colonist alike, was reduced to eating "hides that they had and the straps of the carts, preparing them for food by soaking . . . and roasting them in the fire with maize, and boiling them with herbs and roots."[31] In 1671 a great pestilence carried off many people and livestock. By 1672 the nomadic Apaches and Navajos, also pinched by dwindling food supplies, increased their raids on the settled areas and brought more ruin. One of the Spaniards' feudal promises had always been to protect their charges from such raids; now that promise was seen for what it was worth. By 1675 at least six pueblos had been wiped out, and most others were in desperate straits.[32]

In the light of such conditions it is not surprising to see that the Pueblos began to abandon Spanish habits and return to their folkways. In the past they had been willing to accept the advantages of Spanish technology and even the externals of the new religion, as long as imported items served material and social ends. When missionaries insisted that acceptance of Christianity forbade any retention of aboriginal beliefs and required denial of native rituals, there were probably some opportunists willing to go even that far. But when all of them realized that the new ways were no better than the old ones in bringing rain, curing disease or preventing invasions — indeed, when they seemed to be the cause of so much suffering — then a massive return to the more trusted patterns of ancient teaching was in the offing.

Ironically enough, at the same time Indian practices were being revitalized, the Spanish mounted an energetic campaign to extinguish them altogether. Relations between church and state had been stormy throughout most of the century, but in the person of Juan Francisco de Treviño, arriving as governor sometime after 1670, the missionaries finally found a civil magistrate willing to enforce their suppression of native religion with wholehearted cooperation.[33] As the Indians were moving in one direction, Spanish forces tried with increasing brutality to move them toward the opposite pole. In 1675 forty-seven ceremonial leaders were arrested. Three were hanged, another committed suicide, and the others were released after being whipped only because the Indians made a show of force. Plans for a wider and more effective revolt were not long in forthcoming, and most of the central figures, including el Popé, came from among those leaders publicly humiliated.

The fighting of 1680 caught the Spanish by surprise, and their evacuation left the Indians free to follow pre-contact standards of conduct as they wished. There was an abortive attempt to reconquer the land in 1682, but for the better part of fifteen years the Pueblos had little molestation from soldiers or friars. New Mexico was conquered again by 1696, and Indian resistance took two new forms. Thousands moved west to live with a similar but more remote culture, the Hopi; those who stayed in the river valleys compartmentalized their lives into outward conformity to the dominant culture and inner loyalty to their own.

In piecing together the best possible historical interpretation of these events it is important to notice that political, economic and personal factors did play a role, but they do not tell the whole story. The cultural antagonism between Spaniard and Pueblo had fundamentally religious roots, and an adequate understanding of the 1680 hostilities must give them priority. In the last analysis the Indian war was an attempt to preserve the kind of life which they thought the gods had ordained and which aliens were obviously destroying. The tribes united voluntarily to expel the Spanish because their coercive tactics were preventing a life based on true beliefs and conduct — an ethos seen not only as proper, but as the one way to stave off the disease and famine confronting them. The Pueblo Revolt was an act of people de-termined to reject Christian civilization because it posed a direct threat to their culture and religion, to their integrated structures which embodied indispensable elements for Pueblo survival.[34]

This study of a particular cultural conflict may be useful in shedding more light on one set of concrete historical circumstances and in providing a more comprehensive interpretation of all the facts that were in operation there. But it stands as only one case study in a field that needs a great deal of attention. Historians are now in a position to capitalize on sophisticated treatments of religion in cultural contexts and blend them with more stan-dard surveys of missionary activity. The day has come when we can adjust one-sided interpretations of red-white relations, correcting them with a wealth of new material and a more comprehensive understanding of Indian life. This new awareness is the key to better history of hundreds of cultures whose integrity and richness we are just beginning to appreciate. Once this is under way, the scope and quality of Christian missions can be more real-istically viewed within specific contexts.

Notes

1. The main strength of the contribution made by certain anthropologists is in the way religion can be viewed not as abstract rationalization of ideas and symbols but rather as an effective element in the culture where it flourishes. One of the best statements of this useful viewpoint is the following:

> In anthropology, it has become customary to refer to the collection of notions a people has of how reality is at base put together as their world view. Their general style of life, the way they do things and like to see things done, we usu-ally call their ethos. It is the office of religious symbols . . . to link these in such a way that they mutually confirm one another. Such symbols render the world view believable and the ethos justifiable, and they do it by invoking each in support of the other. The world view is believable because the ethos, which grows out of it, is felt to be authoritative; the ethos is justifiable because the world view, upon which it rests, is held to be true.

See Clifford Geertz, *Islam Observed: Religious Development in Morocco and Indonesia* (New Haven: Yale University Press, 1969), p. 97. For other instructive discussions see Emile Durkheim, *The Elementary Forms of the Religious Life* (New York: Free Press, 1965, fifth printing), pp. 463–64; Robert Redfield, *The Primitive World and Its Trans-formations* (Ithaca: Cornell University Press, 1953), p. 14; Robert N. Bellah, *Toku-gawa Religion: The Values of Pre-Industrial Japan* (Glencoe, Illinois: Free Press, 1957), pp. 59–60; Robert N. Bellah, "Religious Systems," in E. Z. Vogt and E. M. Albert, eds., *People of Rimrock: A Study of Values in Five Cultures* (Cambridge, Massachusetts: Harvard University Press, 1967), p. 227; Clifford Geertz, "Ethos, World-View and the Analysis of Sacred Symbols," *Antioch Review* 19 (December 1957): 424–25; Clifford Geertz, "Religion as a Cultural System," in M. Banton, ed., *Anthropological Approaches to the Study of Religion* (London: Tavistock Publications, 1966), pp. 3–4, 40–41; and

Alfonso Ortiz, "Ritual Drama and the Pueblo World View," in A. Ortiz, ed., *New Perspectives on the Pueblos* (Albuquerque: University of New Mexico Press, 1972), p. 136.

2. This is one possible methodological problem which the student must face. It does not however, present insuperable difficulties when he studies peoples who place(d) strong emphasis on the cohesion and continuity of their culture's values. Many groups of Indians of the American Southwest are striking in this regard and therefore are not likely to have changed substantially between the sixteenth century and our own. For discussions of the problem, see William N. Fenton, *American Indian and White Relations to 1830: Needs and Opportunities for Study* (Chapel Hill: University of North Carolina Press, 1957; reprint New York, 1971) and Edward P. Dozier, "Making Inferences from the Present to the Past," in W. A. Longacre, ed., *Reconstructing Prehistoric Pueblo Societies* (Albuquerque: University of New Mexico Press, 1970), pp. 202–13.

3. It is wise to remind ourselves that we are involved in studying vigorous, living cultures in a specific context. We are not trying to move from this data to generalizations about the processes of acculturation, alienation or compartmentalization. The aims of this essay are not to produce theory in either sociology or theology. This self-conscious limitation has the value of following the concrete orientation of historical studies.

4. This is always a problem for historians in every field, but as long as modern evidence and new insights correspond to the activities and statements of people at the time, one can use more recent categories to advantage and not distort the factual identity of past events.

5. For the best estimates on population distribution, see Edward H. Spicer, *Cycles of Conquest: The Impact of Spain, Mexico and the United States on the Indians of the Southwest, 1533–1960* (Tucson: University of Arizona Press, 1962), pp. 153–55; Edward P. Dozier, "Rio Grande Pueblos," in E. H. Spicer, ed., *Perspectives in American Indian Culture Change* (Chicago: University of Chicago Press, 1961), pp. 99, 136; and Albert H. Schroeder, "Rio Grande Ethnohistory," in A. Ortiz, ed., *New Perspectives on the Pueblos*, p. 48.

For the fascinating and still puzzling story of attempts to abandon the mission and then to secure royal support, see George P. Hammond, "Don Juan de Oñate and the Founding of New Mexico," *New Mexico Historical Review* (hereafter cited as *NMHR*) 2 (April 1927): 139–41, 175–77; issued as a single volume, Santa Fe, 1927. See also France V. Scholes and Lansing B. Bloom, "Friar Personnel and Mission Chronology, 1598–1629," *NMHR* 19 (October 1944): 329–30; Frank D. Reeve, *History of New Mexico* (New York: Lewis Historical Publishing Company, 1961), 1:137–39; Edgard L. Hewett and Reginald Fisher, *Mission Monuments of New Mexico* (Albuquerque: University of New Mexico Press, 1943), p. 74; and Lansing B. Bloom, "Fray Estevan de Perea's *Relacion*," *NMHR* 8 (July 1933): 221–22. The last mentioned author summarizes the government's activities in the following manner:

> . . . it must be acknowledged that they poured out, during the seventeenth century hundreds of thousands of pesos from which they could expect no commensurate material returns. Perhaps it was not pure altruism . . . , and doubtless the Spanish monarchs counted on rich stores of spiritual treasures being laid up to their credit from the work of the church. But the point is that missionary work in New Mexico could not have been carried on without the financial support of the king, and that support was given in astonishing measure.

6. Hubert H. Bancroft, *History of Arizona and New Mexico* (San Francisco: The History Company, 1889), pp. 133–34; Hammond, "Oñate and the Founding of New Mexico," pp. 98–99; and Edward H. Spicer, "Political Incorporation and Cultural Change in New Spain: A Study in Spanish-Indian Relations," in H. Peckham and C. Gibson, eds., *Attitudes of Colonial Powers toward the American Indian* (Salt Lake City: University of Utah Press, 1969), p. 124. This last reference points out that much more than Christianity confronted the Indians. While the friars were preaching, the times were also characterized by "the introduction of the standard institutions of Spanish dominance, namely, encomienda, repartimiento and tribute, corregimiento, missions and ecclesiastical tribunals, the Spanish town, and the Spanish blueprint for reorganization of Indian communities."

7. For highly inflated figures, see the report in F. W. Hodge, G. P. Hammond and A. Rey, eds., *Fray Alonso de Benavides' Revised Memorial of 1634* (Albuquerque: University of New Mexico Press, 1945), pp. 35, 99. More sensible estimations can be found in Scholes and Bloom, "Friar Personnel," p. 330; Reeve, *History of New Mexico,* 1:146–47; France V. Scholes, "Documents for the History of the New Mexico Missions in the Seventeenth Century," *NMHR* 4 (January 1929): 46–50, 51–58; Spicer, *Cycles of Conquest,* pp. 157–58; Edward P. Dozier, *The Pueblo Indians of North America* (New York: Holt, Rinehart and Winston, Inc., 1970), p. 49 and Bancroft, *Arizona and New Mexico,* pp. 160–61.

8. For the best discussion of this particular aspect, see two essays: France V. Scholes, "Church and State in New Mexico, 1610–1650," *NMHR* 11 and 12 (January 1936 to January 1937) and France V. Scholes, "Troublous Times in New Mexico, 1659–1670," *NMHR* 12 through 16 (April 1937 to July 1941 but not appearing in regular installments; issued as a single volume, Albuquerque, 1942). Reeve, *History of New Mexico,* 1:196, also has a measured analysis.

9. France V. Scholes, "The Supply Service of the New Mexican Missions in the Seventeenth Century," *NMHR* 5 (January 1930): 114 discusses all the ramifications of keeping in touch with a farflung outpost that never became self-sufficient. There is a sample packing list for one of the three-year wagon train expeditions in Benavides' *Revised Memorial of 1634,* pp. 111–22.

10. For some specific examples of personal conflict gleamed from the sketchy records, see Scholes, "Troublous Time" (April 1937): 144 and (October 1937): 408–12. References to earlier, less unified, indications of violence can be found in Bancroft, *Arizona and New Mexico,* pp. 167–68; Ralph E. Twitchell, *The Leading Facts of New Mexican History* (Cedar Rapids, Iowa: Torch Press, 1911), 1:346–47; Reeve, *History of New Mexico,* 1:144–46; Schroeder, "Ethnohistory," p. 55; and the translated documents themselves in C. W. Hackett and C. C. Shelby, eds., *Revolt of the Pueblo Indians of New Mexico and Otermin's Attempted Reconquest, 1680–1682* (Albuquerque: University of New Mexico Press, 1942), 2:299.

12. The primary documents are to be found in Hackett and Shelby, *Revolt,* 1:xxii and 2:298–301. A dated but still useful narrative based on them is Bancroft, *Arizona and New Mexico,* p. 170.

13. Standard accounts of the main events can be found in Charles W. Hackett, "The Revolt of the Pueblo Indians of New Mexico in 1680," *The Quarterly of the Texas State Historical Association* 15 (October 1911): 99–100, 130–31; Twitchell, *Leading Facts,* 1:361; Spicer, *Cycles of Conquest,* p. 163; and Dozier, *Pueblos of North America,* p. 59.

While these deaths of white people are usually called a massacre, the Spaniards' conquest of a single pueblo was often more ruthless in loss of life and property. The reduction of Acoma in 1599 brought death to between 600 and 800 Indians, caused the enslavement of 500 others and the utter destruction of the pueblo; see Reeve, *History of New Mexico,* 1:124–25. Another example taken from many is the reconquest of Sia in 1689 which cost another 600 native lives, many of whom "were burned to death in the flames which destroyed a portion of the pueblo rather than submit to captivity at the hands of the Spaniards." Twitchell, *Leading Facts,* 1:380.

14. Hackett and Shelby, *Revolt,* 1:13 and 2:247–48, 251; Twitchell, *Leading Facts,* 1:368; Bancroft, *Arizona and New Mexico,* p. 184. Some authors like Robert Silverberg, *The Pueblo Revolt* (New York: Weybright and Talley, 1970), p. 132, go so far as to say that the Pueblos even refused to continue using melons, fruit trees, wheat, horses and cattle because of their alien origin. There might have been some sentiment expressed along that line, but I doubt that an eminently practical people would destroy easily assimilable aspects of material culture which could benefit their economy and diet. Until such an overreaching assertion can be substantiated further, it seems more reasonable to place the anger of nativist reaction on human presence, not on objects of the natural order.

15. Schroeder, "Ethnohistory," p. 51; Leslie A. White, "The Pueblo of Santa Ana, New Mexico," *American Anthropologist,* n.s., 44 (October–December 1942): 66; Elsie Clews Parsons, *Pueblo Indian Religion* (Chicago: University of Chicago Press, 1939), 1:453–55, 2:1075.

16. For examples in which Christian doctrines were actually applied to physical needs like rain making, toothache and pregnancy, see *Benavides' Revised Memorial of 1634,* pp. 53, 58; see also Bloom, "Perea's *Relacion,*" p. 233.

17. Edwin E. Sylvest, Jr., "Motifs of Franciscan Mission Theory in Sixteenth Century New Spain Province of the Holy Gospel," (Ph.D. diss., Southern Methodist University, 1970), pp. 114–17, 124, 228–29, 253–54.

18. Spicer, *Cycles of Conquest,* p. 282; Edward P. Dozier, "The American Southwest," in E. B. Leacock and N. O. Lurie, eds., *North American Indians in Historical Perspective* (New York: Random House, 1971), pp. 246–48; Dozier, "Rio Grande Pueblos," p. 126; Reginald G. Fisher, "An Outline of Pueblo Indian Religion," *El Palacio* 44 (1938): 172–73.

19. Some nations, for example the Tewa, have emergence tales where the people first appear by coming from under a lake; others, such as the Keres, mention no lake. But the basic concurrence is an underground origin and ultimate return. For variations of the emergence myth, see Alfonso Ortiz, *The Tewa World: Space, Time and Becoming in a Pueblo Society* (Chicago: University of Chicago Press, 1969), p. 122; Leslie A. White, *The Pueblo of Sia, New Mexico* (Washington: Government Printing Office, 1962), pp. 115–31; Dozier, *Pueblos of North America,* pp. 203–04; and Parsons, *Pueblo Indian Region,* 1:182.

20. White, "Santa Ana," p. 88. See also White, *Sia,* p. 236.

21. Ortiz, *Tewa World,* p. 23; Fisher, "Outline of Pueblo Religion," p. 171. For a striking example of the contrast between these two orientations, see the sermon recorded in Bloom, "Perea's *Relacion,*" pp. 229–30.

22. Some of the main sources for these two paragraphs are White, *Sia,* p. 320; Ortiz, "Ritual Drama and Pueblo World View," pp. 142–43; and Elsie Clews Parsons, *The Pueblo of Jemez* (New Haven: Yale University Press, 1925), pp. 124–25.

23. The best discussions of this significant aspect of Pueblo psychology can be

found in Ortiz, "Ritual Drama and Pueblo World View," pp. 153–54; Wigberto J. Moreno, "The Indians of America and Christianity," *The Americas* 14 (April 1958): 413–14; Florence H. Ellis, "Authoritative Control and the Society System in Jemez Pueblo," *Southwestern Journal of Anthropology* 9 (Winter 1953): 392; Leslie A. White, "The Pueblo of San Felipe," *Memoirs of the American Anthropological Association* 3 (1932): 11, 43; and Parsons, *Pueblo Indian Religion,* 1:107–08.

24. Ortiz, "Ritual Drama and Pueblo World View," p. 145. See also Ortiz, *Tewa World,* pp. 50–56, 123–24; and Parsons, *Pueblo Indian Religion,* 1:63–64.

25. Parsons, *Pueblo Indian Religion,* 1:216; 2:1102.

26. For a concrete example of the strain placed on existing ties in Pueblo communities, see *Benavides' Revised Memorial of 1634,* p. 78.

27. Dozier, *Pueblos of North America,* pp. 151, 200.

28. The best discussion of this essential aspect of Pueblo life is Ortiz, *Tewa World,* pp. 80–81, 98, 103, 127. Other important ones are Dozier, "Rio Grande Pueblos," pp. 112–13; Fisher, "Outline of Pueblo Religion," pp. 176–77; and Parsons, *Jemez,* p. 58.

29. This is the heart of the Pueblo value system in a concrete manifestation, and a great deal of information can be found in Ortiz, *Tewa World,* pp. 98, 104, 116; William Whitman, *The Pueblo Indians of San Ildefonso* (New York: AMS Press, 1969), p. 118; W. Krickeberg, H. Trimborn, W. Muller and O. Zerries, *Pre-Columbian American Religions* (London: Weidenfeld and Nicolson, 1968), p. 206; and Parsons, *Jemez,* pp. 74–75.

30. Hackett and Shelby, *Revolt,* 1:60–61; Bancroft, *Arizona and New Mexico,* p. 14; Twitchell, *Leading Facts,* 1:354–57; Reeve, *History of New Mexico,* 1:249–53; Dozier, "American Southwest," pp. 248–49; Fray Angelico Chavez, "Pohé-yemo's Representative and the Pueblo Revolt of 1680," *NMHR* 42 (April 1967): 86.

31. Hackett and Shelby, *Revolt,* 1:xix. See also Spicer, *Cycles of Conquest,* p. 162.

32. Twitchell, *Leading Facts,* 1:348–50; Reeve, *History of New Mexico,* 1:251–52.

33. Scholes, "Troublous Times," (April 1937): 149, (July 1941): 321–22.

34. Ortiz, "Ritual Drama and Pueblo World View," put it well when he wrote on page 136 that "as long as there is a reasonably good fit between world view and religion, between reality as it is defined and as it is lived, world view can be defined as, in the main, expressive. When there is no longer this fit, we have reactions ranging from millennial dreams to violent revolution, all designed to establish a reasonably integrated life." For a modern example of the tensions between white dominance and Indian ways, with the disastrous results that often follow, see Parsons, *Jemez,* pp. 9, 60.

2. Did Franciscans invite martyrdom?

Ramón A. Gutiérrez

Franciscans and the Pueblo Revolt

From *When Jesus Came, the Corn Mothers Went Away: Marriage, Sexuality, and Power in New Mexico, 1500–1846*

In the previous article, Henry Warner Bowden argues that similarities between Pueblo religion and Christianity were not appreciated by the Franciscans as an avenue for introducing their missionary program. Ramón Gutiérrez, in contrast, portrays Franciscans as skillful manipulators of Indians, whose beliefs the priests understood in general if not in particular. The Franciscans insinuated themselves into Pueblo life, Gutiérrez tells us, by consciously and unconsciously assuming the roles of Pueblo leaders, supplanting some of the chiefs and convincing others to collaborate with them.

In the essay that follows, Gutiérrez looks at the disillusion that overcame some Franciscans when the sweet success of their early years began to sour. Gutiérrez explains how, as early as the 1640s, the Franciscans began to lose authority. He tells us why some dispirited Franciscans invited martyrdom and how the actions of Pueblo rebels spoke loudly of their contempt for Catholicism. As he advances his argument, Gutiérrez also provides a vivid and succinct overview of the events of the Pueblo Revolt.

A native of Albuquerque who did his undergraduate training at the University of New Mexico, Ramón Gutiérrez earned a Ph.D. in Latin American history at the University of Wisconsin, Madison (1980). He is currently the associate chancellor at the University of California, San Diego, and founding chair of its Ethnic Studies Department and Center for the Study of Race and Ethnicity. The essay that follows derives from his innovative and sophisticated prize-winning book *When Jesus Came, the Corn Mothers Went Away: Marriage, Sexuality, and Power in New Mexico, 1500–1846* (1991). In that book, New Mexico Hispanic society emerges as hypocritical and exploitative, but it is Gutiérrez's interpretation of Pueblo culture that has sparked the greatest controversy. Some Pueblo Indians have been offended at his portrayal of Pueblo sexuality and his tendency to homogenize what they see as the heterogeneous cultures of discrete Pueblo communities. They have criticized his reliance on Spanish sources and his failure to consult living informants, decisions that he justifies on the grounds that Spanish sources are the best we have and that oral historical memory does not survive with accuracy for many generations. The controversy points up the difficulties of writing the history of American Indians in general.

Questions for a Closer Reading

1. Why did some Franciscans welcome martyrdom, according to Gutiérrez, and why does he see that as an act of aggression against the Pueblos?

2. How does Gutiérrez demonstrate that some Pueblo leaders resisted before the 1670s?

3. When the crisis of the 1670s led Pueblos to practice their religion openly, how did Spaniards treat them?

4. What religious promises did Popé make to his followers?

5. What tactics did Pueblos employ to defeat the better-armed Spaniards?

6. What evidence does Gutiérrez offer of Pueblo rebels' contempt for Catholicism?

Franciscans and the Pueblo Revolt

Franciscan Theocracy

By the mid-1640s it had become clear to many Indians that the Franciscans were no longer the supermen they had once seemed. The novelty of their gifts had worn off and their magic had proven ineffectual in producing rain, health, prosperity, and peace. As some of the original mission personnel died and younger, less experienced friars replaced them, the charisma with which the initial friars had established their authority as town chiefs did not easily transfer over and only fed village factionalism. Given that native hunting and warfare had been supplanted with the arrival of European herds and armaments, it fell to the medicine men to reestablish harmony in the cosmos, to call the ancient gods anew, and to rid the area of the witches (that is, the friars) who had stolen their hearts.

It did not take the fathers long to discover that their children had reverted to idolatry, were invoking the devil, and were clandestinely wallowing in the forbidden pleasures of the flesh. They responded as any father would have with disobedient children — punishments began. None of the backsliders was spared the whip, and some even were beaten to death out of fatherly love. In 1655, for example, Fray Salvador de Guerra discovered that a Hopi Indian named Juan Cuna had been worshipping idols. Guerra viciously whipped Juan until "he was bathed in blood." A second beating was inflicted later that day inside the church. Juan Cuna died in flames that surely resembled those of hell, for when the beating was done, the friar drenched him from head to foot with burning turpentine. Father Guerra

Ramón A. Gutiérrez, *When Jesus Came, the Corn Mothers Went Away: Marriage, Sexuality, and Power in New Mexico, 1500–1846* (Stanford: Stanford University Press, 1991), 127–37.

justified this sort of punishment to ecclesiastical authorities as necessary to abolish idolatry. He stated that several other Indians had received similar treatment, a statement corroborated in 1663 by Nicolás de Aguilar, and by those survivors who were permanently "marked by the burns."[1]

As the Franciscans lost their grip over the Indians and their punishments only bred more hatred, they found themselves isolated and increasingly turned within themselves to find comfort in God, yearning for his tender kisses, wishing that his love would pierce their hearts. Through preaching they had begotten many spiritual children, but only prayer and meditation would nurture their own souls. "Spiritual children . . . are dear and precious," St. Bernard had said, "but the kisses of the spouse are infinitely more agreeable. It is a good thing to save several souls, but it is much sweeter to be with the Word."[2]

The Franciscans had spent years preaching to the Indians, but their labor largely had been for naught. Now, to prove how much they really loved the Indians, they prepared themselves to offer the perfect example of that love, their own deaths through martyrdom. The desire for martyrdom had been a burning drive among many of the friars who entered New Mexico. In fact, 49 of the hundred or so friars who served in New Mexico during the seventeenth century died as martyrs, suffering pains not unlike those they meted out to the Indians. Fray Juan de Escalona traveled to New Mexico in the early 1600s because in a vision he had seen his martyr's crown there. Escalona's confessor tells us that one afternoon while the friar was enraptured praying the Ave Maria, he suddenly shouted out, "Beati primi, beati primi" ("blessed are the first"). Asked what he had seen, Escalona explained:

> Yesterday afternoon, when we were praying the Ave Maria, God our Lord revealed . . . to me that some religious of my father, Saint Francis . . . are to be martyred [in New Mexico]. These religious appeared before me and I saw them being martyred in spirit, and because I was joyful to see them suffer martyrdom with so much spirit and courage, I said: Beati primi, Beati primi.

Escalona reached New Mexico but despite his tireless efforts to convert Indians, reports of his prayer-induced levitations, and frequent visitations by Saint Francis, he died of natural causes and was buried at Santo Domingo Pueblo.[3]

Mother María de Jesús Coronel (1602–65), abbess of the Franciscan convent at Agreda, Burgos, spiritual confidant to King Philip IV, and an avid patroness of New Mexico's missions, inspired several of her devotees to travel to New Mexico in search of martyrdom, claiming that she had led several Franciscans to their deaths there. Mother María said that between 1620 and 1631, she had traveled to New Mexico "three and four times" a day with Saint Michael and Saint Francis as her wings. And because of the many wounds she received from the Pueblo Indians, the "heavenly angels crowned her, wherefore she attained martyrdom from our Lord."[4]

In 1670 Fray José Trujillo arrived in New Mexico, culminating a lifelong quest for martyrdom that had begun in Spain in 1634. Father Trujillo had traveled to the Philippines, to Japan, to Mexico, and finally to New Mexico. It was in Manila in 1649, while conferring with Mother Juana de San Antonio, a nun widely renowned for her holiness and mystical flights, that he learned the location of his martyr's crown. The venerable mother asked Trujillo if he sought martyrdom. "Yes," he said. "Know that it is not here but in New Mexico that God our Lord will satisfy your desires." A decade after Trujillo reached the Rio Grande Valley he was clubbed to death by the Zuñi Indians. Finally he got the mystical marriage he so desired.[5]

Like innocent lambs being led to the slaughter, the Franciscans were "anxious to suffer martyrdom for God," and frequently fantasized about their impending deaths. Friars Juan de Padilla, Luís de Ubeda, and Juan de la Cruz, to name but a few, rushed into adversity hoping to die as fools for Christ. The hagiographers tell us that these men "did not fear turning their backs to hazards . . . or baring their chests to risks, but rather endangered their lives for the salvation of souls." When these martyrdoms became known, said Fray Alonso de Benavides in 1630, "it caused very fervent desires in many to imitate them." Fearlessly the friars exposed themselves to danger knowing that the pains of torture were momentary while those of hell were eternal. Faithful unto death, they uttered the words of their redeemer: "whoever loses his life for my sake and the gospel's will preserve it" (Mark 8:35). Fray Francisco de Porras was killed by the Hopi on June 28, 1633, "to the great sorrow of all," says his biographer, "but to his own great joy because he had attained the goal he sought." Fray Roque de Figueredo too "found life in Christ which he [was] determined to lose in love for him." Though Zuñi's warriors heaped all sorts of insults on him, he did not cower, for "his desire to die triumphantly was greater than his fear of the fatal blow at the hands of the barbarous Indians." Fray Francisco Letrado likewise awaited his persecutors joyfully. With crucifix in hand, as the manuals on martyrdom instructed, Letrado uttered words that "would benefit the souls of bystanders." As the Indians' treacherous arrows pierced his body, he must have thought those things that he was taught to visualize at the moment of death: the Passion of Christ, and Mary and many angels awaiting his soul with a crown in their hands. Bear in mind that though the martyrdoms of these Franciscans may appear like supreme acts of pacifism, they were, quite the contrary, supreme acts of aggression. The Indians were provoked to murder only when they were pushed beyond their human limits. More to the point, the Spanish soldiers always retaliated with brute force whenever the Indians killed their friars. For the friars, then, the means justified their ends.[6]

The Pueblo Revolt and Its Aftermath

The years 1666 to 1670 were marked by drought and meager maize production. Famine swept the land in 1670, and a decade of pestilence and death followed. The Indian population, which in 1638 had totaled roughly 40,000, by 1670 had fallen to 17,000. To complicate matters, in 1672 hordes of hungry Apaches and Navajos in similarly desperate straits began attacking the kingdom's settlements with unprecedented regularity, killing and stealing, and carrying off whatever food they found. The Puebloans' discontent hardly needed stoking. For years they had resented the Spanish, and now they spoke openly of rebellion. The medicine men told their tribesmen that the reason they suffered so was because their ancient gods were angry. If they offered the katsina gifts and respect, they would surely bless them with rainfall, fertility, and happiness. The first group to openly defy colonial rule were the Tewa, the Indians who had had the closest contact with the Spaniards during the seventeenth century. In 1673 they publicly performed prohibited dances, making offerings to their gods and begging them to return. The medicine men worked feverishly, placing hexes on the Christians and stealing their hearts. Apparently their magic worked. In 1675 alone, Indian witchcraft was blamed for sending seven friars and three settlers to their graves.[7]

Ominous forebodings of events to come were everywhere. In 1672, the Jumano Indians of Abó Pueblo revolted, burning their church and murdering Fray Pedro de Avila y Ayala. Before killing Father Pedro with blows from their tomahawks, the Indians stripped him, placed a rope around his neck, and cruelly flogged him. His naked body was found hugging a cross and an image of the Blessed Virgin Mary. In an act symbolic of the death-blow the Indians believed they had given Christ and the Trinity, three lambs whose throats had been slashed were placed at the martyr's feet. The message was unequivocal. Yet one friar read it as saying that the Franciscans were "like lambs among wolves, and these three lambs gave testimony that the dead father was a lamb." Three years later, in 1675, the Virgin Mary of Toledo appeared to a sickly New Mexican girl, cured her illness, and ordered her to "arise and announce to this custody that it will soon be destroyed for the lack of reverence that it shows its priests." The Virgin's apparition sparked a flurry of high Masses throughout the province and prompted Fray Juan de Jesús to urge his brother at San Diego de Jémez Mission to cease construction on the colaterals he was building on the church's nave. Time would be spent best "uniting ourselves with God and preparing to die for our Holy Faith," Fray Juan de Jesús advised, "for the colaterals will soon end in the ashes and many of us in death."[8]

Governor Juan Francisco Treviño, who had arrived in the province in 1675, dealt with the widespread Indian sedition by launching a campaign against idolatry. At Nambé, San Felipe, and Jémez he had known "sorcerers" hung. Forty-seven medicine men who admitted practicing witchcraft were arrested, flogged, and sold into slavery. Before these men could be taken out of the kingdom, the Tewa, armed with clubs and shields, descended on Santa Fe demanding that Treviño release them, threatening to kill him and all the colonists if he refused. The governor pleaded: "Wait a while, children, I will give them to you and pardon them on condition that you forsake idolatry and iniquity." The Indians stood firm. Treviño capitulated.[9]

The confrontation between Treviño and the Tewa over the medicine men indicated how radicalized and defiant the Puebloans had become. One of the men who felt the sting of Treviño's whip was Popé, a San Juan medicine man. Convinced that the yoke of subjugation could no longer be tolerated, Popé moved from San Juan to Taos, the northernmost pueblo, to escape the governor's watchful eye and to plot a provincewide revolt. At Taos, Popé conferred with the caciques of the surrounding pueblos, with the war chiefs who had been marginalized by the superior force of the Spaniards, and with Pueblo dissidents who had escaped the missions' tyranny and taken refuge among the Apaches.

Popé's genius lay in his brilliant organizational skills and his ability to inflame the popular imagination through the millenarianism he articulated. He told the disaffected, the hungry, and the displaced that their ancient gods would not return bearing gifts of happiness and prosperity until the Christians and their God were dead. Then their sadness and misery would end, for they would be as they had been at the time of emergence from the underworld. "They would gather large crops of grain, maize with large and thick ears, many bundles of cotton, many calabashes and watermelons," and would enjoy abundant health and leisure. To those elders and chiefs who had been flayed by the friars for their polygamous marriages, or sheared of their hair as fornicators, Popé promised that "who shall kill a Spaniard will get an Indian woman for a wife, and he who kills four will get four women, and he who kills ten or more will have a like number of women." To a people who had seen their agricultural lands usurped and their tribute payments grow onerous over time, Popé offered liberation. When the Spaniards were all dead, he promised, they would "break the lands and enlarge their cultivated fields . . . free from the labor they performed for the religious and the Spaniards."[10]

From Taos Pueblo, Popé sent messengers throughout the kingdom

announcing that if the people respected the katsina and called them properly, they would return to usher in a new age. Popé himself regularly called
Caudi, Tilini, and Tleume, the katsina who lived in the kiva of the Taos
medicine society but "never came out." Finally, after many prayers and offerings, the katsina came out "emit[ting] fire from all the extremities of
their bodies." They told Popé that "they were going underground to the
lake of Copala" and would return after the Spaniards were gone. The
katsina showed Popé how to defeat the Christians and gave him a knotted
cord, which he was to circulate to all the pueblos. Those villages that wished
to join the rebellion were to untie one knot as a sign of obedience, and by
the others would count the days to revolt.[11]

Popé enlisted the caciques of Taos, Picuris, San Lorenzo, Santo Domingo, Jémez, and Pecos, as well as a number of prominent mixed-bloods:
Domingo Naranjo from Santa Clara, Nicolás Jonva from San Ildefonso, and
Domingo Romero from Tesuque. They met secretly each time a village cele-
brated its saint's feast day so that their travel to and fro would not provoke
suspicion. August 11, 1680, the first night of the new moon, was chosen as
the date for the revolt. They knew the settlers would be most vulnerable to
attack right before the triennial supply caravan arrived from Mexico City in
mid-September with ammunition and horses.[12]

On August 9, 1680, Popé dispatched two messengers to all the pueblos
with knotted cords indicating that only two days remained. They told the
caciques that a letter from Po-he-yemu, "the father of all the Indians, their
great captain, who had been such since the world had been inundated," had
arrived from the north informing that "all of them . . . should rebel, and that
any pueblo that would not agree to it they would destroy, killing all the
people."[13]

The caciques of Tanos, San Marcos, and La Cienega opposed the rebellion, and on August 9 informed Governor Antonio de Otermín of its impending approach. Otermín had Popé's messengers arrested and tortured
until they revealed what the knotted cords meant. Tesuque's Indians
learned of this, and fearing that all might be lost immediately dispatched
runners to the confederated pueblos informing them that they should rebel
the next day.[14]

August 10, 1680, began for Fray Juan Pío like any Sunday morning. He
left Santa Fe on foot to say Mass at Tesuque, accompanied by his armed es-
cort, Pedro Hidalgo. But on this day the pueblo was totally deserted. The
friar searched everywhere for the Indians and finally found them a few
miles outside the village armed and wearing war paints. "What is this, children, are you mad?," the friar asked. "Do not disturb yourselves; I will help
you and will die a thousand deaths for you." Before he could say anything
else, a shower of arrows pierced his breast. Pedro Hidalgo would have been
killed too had he not been on his horse. He barely escaped, and by ten that

morning was back in Santa Fe reporting to the governor. All day emissaries from every part of the kingdom arrived in Santa Fe telling of the massacres they had seen. The Indians' fury had struck the entire province like a bolt of lightning. In one moment a century's work seemed destroyed.[15]

The revolt proceeded as Popé had instructed. First the Indians stole or killed "the principal nerve of warfare," the horses and mules, which the Spaniards had introduced into the province and which had been so instrumental in the conquest and subordination of the Puebloans. Without these beasts of burden, the Spaniards were helpless against mounted Pueblo and Apache warriors. Without horses the Spanish could not communicate rapidly with the centers of authority in New Spain. Indian runners could outrun and outstalk any settler. Whatever technological advantages the Spaniards had on account of their armaments, the Indians offset in numbers. Against roughly 170 colonists capable of bearing arms stood 8,000 or more Indian warriors; a ratio of approximately 1 to 50.[16]

Once the horses were in Indian hands, Popé's forces isolated the settlements in the northern half of the kingdom (the Rio Arriba) from those in the southern half (the Rio Abajo). In the north, all roads to Santa Fe were blocked, and one by one the Spanish settlements were pillaged and razed by the Indians, who scavenged whatever armaments they could. In a few hours 401 settlers and 21 friars were killed. Those who survived gathered at the governor's residence in Santa Fe. The colonists of the Rio Abajo gathered at Isleta.[17]

By August 13, all of the villages in the Rio Arriba had been destroyed and only Santa Fe stood, surrounded by Pueblo and Apache warriors who were ready for a final assault. Grossly outnumbered but stubbornly refusing to admit defeat, Otermín made one last peace overture. Through Juan, a Tano Indian servant turned rebel leader, Otermín implored the caciques "that even though they had committed so many atrocities, still there was a remedy, for if they would return to obedience to his Majesty they would be pardoned." The chiefs jeered and demanded through Juan that

> all classes of Indians who were in our power be given up to them, both those in the service of the Spaniards and those of the Mexican nation of that suburb of Analco. He demanded also that his wife and children be given up to him, and likewise that all the Apache men and women whom the Spaniards had captured in war be turned over to them, inasmuch as some Apaches who were among them were asking for them.

Otermín refused, and the battle for Santa Fe began.[18]

For nine days Santa Fe lay under siege. To hasten the colonists' surrender, the rebels cut off their food and water. By August 20th the Indians sensed victory. That night they were heard shouting gleefully: "Now the God of the Spaniards, who was their father, is dead, and Santa María, who was their mother, and the saints . . . were pieces of rotten wood" and that "their own God whom they obeyed [had] never died." Determined that it was better "to die fighting than of hunger and thirst," the colonists at Santa Fe marshalled all their firepower for a final assault on the morning of August 21. The strategy worked. Popé's forces quickly lost 350 men and temporarily were set to flight. At day's end, Otermín and the settlers decided to abandon Santa Fe before the Indians recouped their losses and returned to rout them. Otermín hoped that he would be able to join forces with the settlers of the Rio Abajo, whom he thought were still gathered at Isleta, and return north with them to subdue the apostates. But unbeknownst to him, the refugees at Isleta had already fled south toward El Paso.[19]

The colonists' retreat south from Santa Fe was filled with horrors. In every village they found piles of mutilated bodies strewn amid ashes of still smoldering fires. At Sandía Pueblo the mission's statues were covered with excrement. Two chalices had been discarded in a basket of manure, and the paint on the altar's crucifix had been stripped off with a whip. Feces covered the holy communion table and the arms of a statue of Saint Francis had been hacked off with an ax. At every mission along their route they reported the most unspeakable profanations of Christian *sacra*.[20]

The Christians felt equal revulsion on seeing and hearing of how the friars had died. On that August night of rebellion, the Jémez Indians apprehended Fray Juan de Jesús, bound him naked onto a pig's back and paraded him through the town, heaping all sorts of jeers and blows on him. Then they removed him from the pig, forced him onto his hands and knees and took turns riding atop his back, repeatedly spurring his haunches to prod him forward. When the warriors were ready to kill him, some dissension erupted in their ranks. But showing a fidelity to death and a love for his persecutors that the manuals of martyrdom assured him would win a crown in heaven, Father Juan allegedly said: "Children, I am a poor old man, do not fight, do not kill each other in order to protect me; do what God permits." And so they shoved a sword through his heart and gave him numerous blows. His body was discovered by the Spaniards in some woods near the pueblo.[21]

Though the Christians were aghast at how the Pueblo Indians had manifested their anger, one only has to recall the massive desecration of katsina masks, kivas, and other native sacra that occurred during the Spanish conquest to understand why the Indians retaliated so exactly during the Pueblo Revolt. The tables were now turned in this contest of cultures. The Indians had learned well from their overlords the functions of iconoclasm in political spectacle.

When Otermín's forces finally reached Isleta, the pueblo was deserted. A week earlier, on August 14, news had reached Isleta that all the Spaniards of the Rio Arriba had been killed, and acting on this information, the settlers, under the leadership of Alonso García, had abandoned Isleta and retreated south. The reconquest of New Mexico would have to wait. For the moment, the only succor either refugee group could expect was from the mission supply train they knew was advancing toward New Mexico. News of the revolt reached Fray Francisco de Ayeta's supply caravan on August 25, just south of El Paso. He promptly advanced toward Socorro, and it was near there on September 6 that the Isleta and Santa Fe survivors of the rebellion were finally united. Together they numbered 1,946, of whom approximately 500 were Pueblo and Apache slaves.[22]

The Christians' defeat and departure were cause for great celebration among the Pueblos. Popé and his two captains, Alonso Catiti of Santo Domingo and Luís Tupatu of Picuris, traveled throughout the province ordering everyone to return "to the state of their antiquity, as when they came from the lake of Copola; that this was the better life and the one they desired, because the God of the Spaniards was worth nothing and theirs was very strong." Popé promised that if they lived in accordance with their ancestral laws, there would be endless peace, prosperity, and harmony.[23]

But none of this would be possible so long as there were vestiges of Christianity. Crosses and images of Christ, of the Virgin Mary, and of the saints had to be destroyed. Churches had to be razed and their bells shattered. Men and women were to forget their Christian names and use only native ones. They were to purify themselves by plunging "into the rivers and wash[ing] themselves with amole [a soap-root] . . . washing even their clothing, with the understanding that there would thus be taken from them the character of the holy sacraments." Anyone who spoke Spanish or uttered the name of Jesus or Mary would be punished severely. Men were to abandon the wife they had taken in matrimony "for any one whom they might wish." Everyone was "to burn the seeds which the Spaniards sowed and to plant only maize and beans, which were the crops of their ancestors." All of this was to be done in the presence of the children so that they would learn the ways of the ancients and the meaning of respect.[24]

Within weeks of the Spaniards' defeat, the indigenous sacral topography was restored. "Flour, feathers, and the seed of maguey, maize, and tobacco" were offered to the spirits at pre-conquest shrines. Kivas that had been desecrated and filled with sand were emptied and resacralized. At last the gods who had abandoned their people and allowed them to perish from hunger and sickness returned from the underworld.[25]

The Spanish survivors of the Pueblo Revolt were genuinely confused by what had happened. They thought themselves blameless and self-righteously pinned the entire disaster on the Indians. A visibly shaken

Governor Otermín bristled that the devil had ensnared the Indians with idolatries and superstitions to which "their stupid ignorance predisposes them, for they live blindly in their freedom and stupid vices." In the months that followed, Otermín gleaned the whys of the revolt. Answers came from five Indians he captured. From Pedro Nanboa, an 80-year-old Indian, Governor Otermín learned that for more than 70 years the Indians had resented Spanish rule because the Christians had destroyed their religious objects, had prohibited their ceremonials, and had humiliated and punished their old men. For this reason the Indians "had been plotting to rebel and to kill the Spaniards and the religious . . . planning constantly to carry it out down to the present occasion."[26]

Two Queres Indians voiced more specific complaints. They objected to the "ill treatment and injuries" they had received from Otermín's constables who "would not leave them alone, [had] burned their estufas [kivas]," and constantly beat them. The Queres had wanted to be "free from the labor they had performed for the religious and the Spaniards." They had grown "weary of putting in order, sweeping, heating, and adorning the church." The Tano Indians agreed. They too had "tired of the work they had to do for the Spaniards and the religious, because they did not allow them to plant or do other things for their own needs." Had the Christians shown them respect there might not have been a rebellion, explained Joseph. Instead, "they beat [us], took away what [we] had, and made [us] work without pay."[27]

The Franciscans pondered the Pueblo Revolt and concluded that the only thing they were guilty of was selfless love for the Indians. Fray Antonio de Sierra wondered why it was that "the Indians who have done the greatest harm are those who have been most favored by the religious and who are most intelligent." What seemed to preoccupy the friars most were the martyrdoms their brothers had suffered. These were not a cause for sadness and tears, but a cause for joy. "We do not mourn the blood shed by twenty-one of our brothers," wrote Fray Juan Alvarez, "for from them there comes to our sacred religion such an access of faith and such honor and glory to God and His church." Fray Francisco de Ayeta was similarly philosophical; that "which the world calls losses, they [are] really the richest treasure of the church."[28]

The viceroy, dignitaries of the Franciscan Order in New Spain, and a few survivors of the Pueblo Revolt gathered at the Cathedral of Mexico City on March 1, 1681, to eulogize New Mexico's martyrs. In his sermon, Doctor Ysidro Sariñana y Cuenca, the cathedral's canon, reflected on how a century's work among "wild beasts," teaching them how to cultivate the soil, clothing their nakedness, and showing them how to live in houses, had ended. The arrows that had sapped the lives of the friars were like a "womb pregnant with darts." Their suffering was "the sure road to life; because the better title corresponding to such deaths is to call them lives," said Sariñana. New Mexico's martyrs had perfectly imitated Christ. Like Christ, they had died because of their Father's love for humanity and because of man's hatred and ingratitude. God did not love the sins of the persecutors, but he loved the patience of the persecuted. He did not love the evil hand that wounded, but he loved the suffering of the wounds. When the arrows of treachery had pierced the martyrs' breasts, when tomahawks had crushed their skulls, and when flames had consumed their bodies, they had been united in mystical marriage with God, a true sign of their perfection. No words captured the mood of that day better than those of St. Ignatius of Antioch: "I am yearning for death with all the passion of a lover. Earthly longings have been crucified; in me there is left no spark of desire for mundane things, but only a murmur of living water that whispers within me, 'Come to Father.'"[29]

Notes

1. France V. Scholes, *Troublous Times in New Mexico, 1659–1670* (Albuquerque: Historical Society of New Mexico Publications in History), 1942, pp. 12–13. Declaration of Nicolás de Aguilar, May 11, 1663, AGN-INQ 512:99. Inga Clendinnen found a similar pattern of violence at the Franciscan mission of Yucatán. See "Disciplining the Indians."

2. St. Bernard, "Canticle of Canticles," 85:13, quoted in Robley E. Whitson, *Mysticism and Ecumenism* (New York, 1966), pp. 84–85.

3. J. M. Espinosa, *Crusaders of the Rio Grande: The Story of Don Diego de Vargas and the Reconquest and Refounding of New Mexico* (Chicago, 1942), p. 15. Zárate Salmerón, Fray Jeronimo, *Relaciones* (Albuquerque, 1966), pp. 99–100. Fray Agustin de Vetancurt, *Teato Mexicano: Descripcion breve de los sucessos exemplare de la Nueva Espana en el Nuevo Mundo,* 4 vols. (Madrid, 1961), vol. 4, pp. 171–73.

4. Fredrick W. Hodge, George P. Hammond, and Agapito Rey, eds. and trans., *Fray Alonso de Benavides' Revised Memorial of 1634* (Albuquerque, 1945), pp. 140, 142. (Hereafter RBM.) María de Jesús Coronel's life is best studied in H. Thurston, *Surprising Mystics* (Chicago, 1955), pp. 122–32; "Sor María de Agreda," *Diccionario Enciclopédico Hispano-Americano* (Barcelona, 1887), vol. 1, p. 603; M. Agreda, *Cartas de la Madre Sor María de Agreda y del Rey Don Felipe IV* (Madrid, 1885–86), 2 vols. Mother María's *Mystical City of God* was widely read in Europe and America, and was published in more than a hundred editions. This book is an account of the life of the Blessed Virgin Mary as dictated to Mother María by the Virgin herself, including her thoughts while still in St. Anne's womb and details of St. Anne and St. Joachim's sex lives. For these heterodox ideas Mother María was prosecuted by the Inquisition. See her *Mystica Ciudad de Dios* (Madrid, 1742), vol. 1, pp. 10, 240–54, 350–66.

5. Fray Agustín de Vetancurt, *Teatro Mexicano: Descripción breve de los sucessos exemplares de la Nueva España en el Nuevo Mundo* (Madrid, 1961), 4 vols., vol. 4,

pp. 228–32. (Hereafter TM.) James B. Defouri, *The Martyrs of New Mexico: A Brief Account of the Lives and Deaths of the Earliest Missionaries in the Territory* (Las Vegas, N.M., 1893), pp. 53–58.

6. *RBM,* pp. 50–56, 77, 219, 221; Adolph F. Bandelier, "Fray Juan de Padilla, the First Catholic Martyr in Eastern Kansas, 1542," *American Catholic Quarterly Review* 15 (1890): 551–65; Defouri, *The Martyrs of New Mexico,* pp. 1–24, 26–27. *TM,* vol. 3, p. 264. *TM,* vol. 4, pp. 174–75. For a comparative analysis of Christian martyrdoms in Japan, see Charles R. Boxer, *The Christian Century in Japan, 1549–1650* (Berkeley, Calif., 1951), pp. 340–57, and George Elison, *Deus Destroyed: The Image of Christianity in Early Modern Japan* (Cambridge, Mass., 1973).

7. Petition of Fray Francisco de Ayeta, May 10, 1679, Charles W. Hackett, ed. and trans., *Historical Documents Relating to New Mexico, Nueva Vizcaya, and Approaches Thereto, 1773* (Washington, D.C., 1937), vol. 3, p. 302 (hereafter HD); *RBM,* p. 292.

8. *TM,* vol. 4, pp. 286–87; *RBM,* p. 292; Defouri, *The Martyrs of New Mexico,* pp. 35–37; Petition of Fray Francisco de Ayeta, May 10, 1679, *HD,* p. 298. Various authors—Vetancurt, Benavides, Defouri—claim that Fray Pedro de Avila y Ayala was killed at Hawikuh. Fray Francisco de Ayeta said that Fra Pedro died at Abó, and since the two men were in New Mexico at the same time, I have accepted his account as true. *TM,* vol. 3, pp. 274, 281–82.

9. Declarations of Luís de Quintana and Diego López, 1681, Charles W. Hackett, ed., *Revolt of the Pueblo Indians of New Mexico and Otermín's Attempted Reconquest, 1680–1682* (Albuquerque, 1942), vol. 2, pp. 289–90, 300. (Hereafter RPI.) Declaration of Diego López, 1681, *RPI,* vol. 2, p. 301.

10. Declaration of Jerónimo, a Tigua Indian, January 1, 1682, *RPI,* vol. 2, p. 361. Declaration of Pedro García, a Tagno Indian, August 25, 1680, *RPI,* vol. 1, pp. 24–25. Declaration of Pedro Naranjo, a Queres Indian, December 19, 1681, *RPI,* vol. 2, pp. 246–47.

11. Declaration of Pedro Naranjo, a Queres Indian, 1681, *RPI,* vol. 2, p. 246.

12. Ibid.; Declaration of Luís de Quintana, 1681, *RPI,* vol. 2, p. 295; J. Sando, "The Pueblo Revolt," in William G. Sturtevant, general editor, *Handbook of North American Indians* (Washington, D.C., 1979), vol. 9, 195 (hereafter HNAI); A. Chávez, "Pohé-yemo's Representative."

13. Declaration of Luís de Quintana, 1681, *RPI,* vol. 2, p. 295; Otermín Autos, August 9, 1680, *RPI,* vol. 1, pp. 4–5.

14. Otermín Autos, August 9–10, 1680, *RPI,* vol. 1, pp. 1–6.

15. Declaration of Pedro Hidalgo, August 10, 1680, *RPI,* vol. 1, pp. 6–7. Otermín Autos, August 10, 1680, *RPI,* vol. 1, pp. 7–9.

16. Opinion of Cabildo, September 14, 1680, *RPI,* vol. 1, p. 120. Letter of Fray Francisco de Ayeta, 1679, *HD,* p. 299.

17. Otermín Autos, October 9, 1680, *RPI,* vol. 1, pp. 194–95; Muster, September 29, 1680, *RPI,* vol. 1, pp. 134–53.

18. Otermín to Fray Francisco de Ayeta, September 8, 1680, *RPI,* vol. 1, pp. 98–101.

19. Declaration of Josephe, Spanish-speaking Indian, December 19, 1681, *RPI,* vol. 2, pp. 239–40; Otermín Autos, August 13–20, 1680, *RPI,* vol. 1, p. 13. Otermín Autos, August 13–21, 1680, *RPI,* vol. 1, p. 15. Certification of departure, August 21, 1680, *RPI,* vol. 1, p. 19.

20. Opinion of the Santa Fe Cabildo, October 3, 1680, *RPI,* vol. 1, pp. 177–78.

21. Fray Ysidro Sariñana y Cuenca, *The Franciscan Martyrs of 1680: Funeral Oration*

over the Twenty-one Franciscan Missionaries Killed by the Pueblo Indians, August 10, 1680 (Santa Fe, 1906), p. 16; "Carta del Padre Fray Silvestre de Escalante," April 2, 1778, *Documentos para servir a la historia del Nuevo México, 1538–1778* (Madrid, 1962), pp. 305–24 (hereafter DHNM); J. Manuel Espinosa, *Crusaders of the Rio Grande: The Story of Don Diego de Vargas and the Reconquest and Refounding of New Mexico* (Chicago, 1942), pp. 19–20.

22. France V. Scholes, "Civil Government and Society in New Mexico in the Seventeenth Century," *NMHR* 10 (1935): 96; *RPI*, vol. 1, pp. 21–65.

23. Declaration of Pedro Naranjo, a Queres Indian, December 19, 1681, *RPI*, vol. 2, p. 248.

24. Declaration of Pedro Naranjo, a Queres Indian, December 19, 1681, *RPI*, vol. 2, p. 248. Declaration of Juan, a Tegua Indian, December 18, 1681, *RPI*, vol. 2, p. 235. Declaration of Josephe, Spanish-speaking Indian, December 19, 1681, *RPI*, vol. 2, p. 239; Declaration of Juan Lorenzo, a Queres Indian, December 20, 1681, *RPI*, vol. 2, 251.

25. Declaration of Josephe, a Spanish-speaking Indian, and of Juan Lorenzo, a Queres Indian, December 19–20, 1681, *RPI*, vol. 2, pp. 239–40, 249–52. Declaration of Juan Lorenzo, a Queres Indian, December 20, 1681, *RPI*, vol. 2, p. 251.

26. Otermín Auto, September 13, 1680, *RPI*, vol. 1, 122. Declaration of Pedro Nanboa, an Indian, September 6, 1680, *RPI*, vol. 1, p. 61; Declaration of Pedro García, an Indian, September 6, 1680, *RPI*, vol. 1, p. 62.

27. Declaration of Josephe, Spanish-speaking Indian, December 19, 1681, and Declaration of Juan Lorenzo, a Queres Indian, December 20, 1681, *RPI*, vol. 2, pp. 239–40, 251. Declaration of Pedro Naranjo, a Queres Indian, December 19, 1681, *RPI*, vol. 2, pp. 245–47. Declaration of Juan Lorenzo, a Queres Indian, December 20, 1681, *RPI*, vol. 2, p. 251. Declaration of Pedro García, a Tano Indian, August 25, 1680, *RPI*, vol. 1, pp. 24–25. Declaration of Josephe, Spanish-speaking Indian, December 19, 1681, *RPI*, vol. 2, pp. 239–41.

28. Sierra Letter to Ayeta, September 4, 1680, *RPI*, vol. 1, p. 59. Letter of Friar Juan Alvarez, et al., to viceroy, October 15, 1680, *RPI*, vol. 1, pp. 203–04. Letter of Ayeta to viceroy, August 31, 1680, *RPI*, vol. 1, p. 53.

29. Sariñana y Cuenca, *The Franciscan Martyrs*, pp. 17–18. Maxwell Staniforth, trans. *Early Christian Writings* (Harmondsworth, Eng., 1968), p. 106. I thank Professor Sabine MacCormack for bringing this document to my attention.

Van Hastings Garner

Seventeenth-Century New Mexico, the Pueblo Revolt, and Its Interpreters

In this essay, historian Van Hastings Garner disagrees with earlier historians who see religion as a primary cause of the Pueblo Revolt. Writing in the mid-1970s, and as apparently unaware of Bowden's work as Bowden was of his, Garner argues that Franciscan missionaries tolerated the continuation of Pueblo religious practices and recognized that it would be too much to expect Indians to convert immediately and fully. Franciscans, Garner argues, made Christianity tolerable for Pueblos by allowing them to maintain old beliefs while adopting the outward forms of the new religion (that is, to practice what he terms a "syncretic" religion). Historians, he says, had emphasized "the religious character of the rebellion . . . far out of proportion to its actual relevance."

Garner sees the essential causes of the Pueblo Revolt in immediate events — drought, famine, and Apache raids of the 1670s — the same events that Bowden and Gutiérrez see only as catalysts for a revolt caused by deeper religious and cultural differences. Garner acknowledges the Spaniards' growing intolerance of Pueblo Indian religious practices in the 1670s, but he explains the revolt in material rather than religious terms. When Pueblos ceased to profit by working for Spanish *encomenderos* and missionaries and when Spanish arms could not provide military protection against Apaches, Pueblos rallied around rebel leaders as they never had before. Thanks to their "acculturation" to the ways of Spaniards, Pueblos had knowledge of horses and guns that facilitated their victory. If the rebels seemed to focus their hatred on priests and religious objects, Garner concludes, it was simply because "the Church was the focal point of Spanish-Indian contact," not because the Pueblos repudiated Christianity. To the contrary, he argues, the Pueblos' syncretic religion, with its Christian elements, remained intact.

Garner also differs with France Scholes's widely accepted view of the nature of social relations in seventeenth-century New Mexico. In the 1930s Scholes had drawn on previously neglected sources, particularly the records of the Inquisition, to portray New Mexico in the 1600s as a place where Franciscans, *encomenderos,* and governors fought bitterly with one another. Their failure to present a united front, Scholes said, weakened their authority in the eyes of Pueblos and contributed to the Pueblo Revolt. Garner disagrees. Drawing heavily on evidence presented by Scholes himself, Garner finds New Mexico a place of relative harmony until the 1670s.

Garner recognizes that Indians had tried to revolt on several occasions in what he sees as a relatively harmonious era before 1670. The revolts failed, Garner explains, because Spaniards remained unified and able to instill fear of military reprisals and because Pueblos remained relatively content and divided among themselves.

Van Hastings Garner completed his doctorate at the University of California, Santa Barbara, in 1972. This article arose out of research he did for his dissertation. He is dean of the College of the Extended University, California State Polytechnic University, Pomona, a position he has held since 1989.

Questions for a Closer Reading

1. In Garner's view, what group wielded the greatest power in New Mexico, civil officials or Franciscans?

2. What is "syncretism" and how does Garner believe it contributed to harmonious relations between Spaniards and Indians?

3. What did missionaries and *encomenderos* have in common, according to Garner?

4. How did Spaniards contribute to a breakdown of Pueblo relations with Athapascan peoples, according to Garner?

5. What does Garner believe Pueblos gained from the presence of Spaniards?

6. Why did Pueblos become disaffected with Spaniards, according to Garner?

7. Why does Garner think that the Pueblos' "acculturation" helped ensure the success of their revolt?

8. Does Garner believe the revolt could have occurred without Popé's leadership?

Seventeenth-Century New Mexico, the Pueblo Revolt, and Its Interpreters[1]

Unfortunately, it is customary to treat seventeenth-century New Mexico as an isolated frontier society with uncomplicated human relationships. Out of this misconception has arisen much confusion regarding New Mexican society and a misunderstanding of the events that led to the Pueblo Revolt of 1680 as well as of the Revolt itself. The ideas set forth by France V. Scholes in his *Church and State in New Mexico 1610–1650* (1937) and *Troublous Times in New Mexico 1659–1670* (1942) offer convincing proof.

According to Scholes, the entire history of seventeenth-century New Mexico revolves around the themes that "the religious and economic motives of empire were antagonistic if not essentially incompatible,"[2] that all the provincial governors were "inspired by consuming self-interest,"[3] and that with few exceptions, these administrative officials were exploiters of people and resources. Nor were the governors the only ones who deserve condemnation; in most cases, Scholes believes, the governors found that "personal gain was best advanced by joining with the colonials in a conscious policy of exploitation."[4] Thus Spanish officialdom collaborated with

Van Hastings Garner, "Seventeenth-Century New Mexico," *Journal of Mexican American History* (1974): 41–70. Garner provided the fuller, more descriptive title used in this book.

the Hispanic population to form a secular community whose main aim was self-aggrandizement, usually at the expense of the Indian. Scholes further condemns the civil population by asserting that they abandoned the governor whenever it appeared to be in their best interests to do so. Adhering to the social and racial attitudes of his day, this historian intimates that the capricious nature of the local population intensified as the mestizo and mulatto grew in number. Fortunately for the reputation of the settlers, however, Scholes hastens to add that "this dark and gloomy picture must not blind us to the fact that there were several important families who were marked out above the rank and file."[5]

Standing against this horde, from Scholes's perspective, were the pious and generally staunch Franciscan friars:

> The Pueblo Indians, their lands and their labor, constituted the chief resources to be utilized and the soldier-settler oppressed them with a heavy hand. The Friars, realizing that exploitation of the Indians would thwart the success of their missionary program, resisted abuses with all the means at their disposal.[6]

While Scholes admits that the Indians sometimes suffered at the hands of the Franciscans, he assures us that most of their suffering was the necessary product of Christianization; if the Franciscans were harsh, it should be attributed to their efforts to stamp out the old ways of the Pueblos.

To Scholes the Indians for the most part were incapable of appreciating the benefits of the new culture. As he sees them:

> The Pueblos were not unwilling to accept the externals of the new faith but found it difficult to understand the deeper spiritual values of Christianity. The burden of labor and tribute might have been tolerated if offset by recognized advantages, but the new faith was no more efficient in guaranteeing a harvest or success in the hunt. What has been gained by accepting Spanish overlordship?[7]

In a sense, then, the Indians were like children in a new world and entrapped in the struggle between the Franciscans and the Hispanic community. Seeing their parents quarreling, the Indians were demoralized and longed for the old times when life was much less complicated.

Unfortunately, the Europeans were also split in their attitude toward the Indian's reaffirmation of his old ways. In Scholes's analysis of the situation, when the Indians began to return to their native culture and to dance their *catzina,* the friars' efforts to eradicate such heathen practices were obstructed by the civil population. As a result of this moral uncertainty and lack of discipline, the children did indeed reject the new culture and made the final break with it in the Pueblo Revolt of 1680. Scholes paternalistically concludes: "We cannot blame them if they were more conscious of present burdens than the spiritual benefits that accrue mostly in the future."[8]

Despite the fact that Scholes's obvious ethnocentrism leads him into several basic errors, it must be acknowledged that his pioneering works[9] did make a substantial contribution to an understanding of New Mexico prior to the Pueblo Revolt of 1680. Also, he proved that seventeenth-century New Mexican history could be written without the New Mexican archives, which were destroyed in the Pueblo Revolt.

Then, too, Scholes had undertaken a sizeable task. As anyone working with the borderlands knows, skimpy documentation fortified by conjecture is often necessary in uncovering the history of the Spanish Southwest. Consequently, Scholes makes some understandable mistakes.

Motivated by a deep love for the pious fathers, relying on the basic assumption that the "religious and economic motives of empire were antagonistic if not essentially incompatible," then driven by a need to moralize and affix blame, Scholes warps the character of the colonial governors. Using admittedly biased sources and citing a few unquestionably corrupt officials, he arrives at his generalization that all of the governors were "inspired by consuming self-interest." As with most men, self-interest was undoubtedly a motivating concern, but the governors were inspired and driven by a variety of other motives, most of which Scholes ignores.

Likewise, Scholes never fully understands his idols, the intrepid Franciscan friars. They did not always stand firm against Pueblo beliefs and culture. As a matter of fact, his friars were capable of making some open-minded and pragmatic decisions in order to solidify a union with the citizen-soldier, whom Scholes claims they were continually resisting.

Scholes's emphasis on a church-and-state theme distorts his analysis of seventeenth-century New Mexico. While at first glance a theme of religious-civil struggle appears to dominate the entire century, and there were many conflicts between Franciscan father and citizen-soldier, the truth of the matter is that both of them needed and relied on each other. The reality of their interdependence is a crucial point to be borne in mind, for its significance weighs heavily in a valid interpretation of New Mexican history in the seventeenth century.

Nor does Scholes ever fully understand the Indians, whom he views from a Spanish perspective. Thus, to this historian the North American aborigine was morally, intellectually, and culturally immature, and most importantly, he was considered to be dependent on the Spaniards for his basic needs.

Scholes's feeling for the Indian was so paternalistic as to elicit a response from Jack Forbes in his work *Apache, Navaho and Spaniard*. Forbes counters

Scholes's description of the Indians with a pan-Indian interpretation. As he sees them, the Indians were hardly childlike figures; instead, they were full-grown men and women struggling to regain the liberty which had been wrenched from them by an imperialistic aggressor. Moreover, Forbes argues that the Athapascans and Pueblos were traditionally friendly and that the long-established cooperation between the two indigenous peoples continued after the Spanish Conquest in spite of the all-out effort of the Spaniards to destroy their good will.

Forbes emphasizes his belief that Spanish overlordship was maintained by cruel repression of an involuntary population. For this analysis of the colonial situation he relies on the assumption that the antagonisms were racial rather than cultural in origin. For this reason he finds it pointless to make differentiation among the various factions within the Spanish community. In Forbes's opinion, the Indians "in spite of harsh persecution by fanatically intolerant Spaniards . . . preserved their ancient religion and beliefs" and began a long struggle "for religious and political freedom."[10] Even the Navaho, traditionally described as a raider and pillager of both European and Pueblo, is rendered in Forbes's interpretation as a crusader against the European.[11]

Although the reader can appreciate the dignity Forbes is trying to give to the Athapascan and Pueblo, there are some critical flaws in his book. In the first place, his entire work is based on an acceptance of the premise (not yet proven) that pan-Indianism was a major theme throughout the period. His view is as pro-Indian as Scholes's is pro-Spaniard. Secondly, while the history of the Athapascan and Pueblo reveals their dignity, the nature of their resistance did not fit the stereotyped struggle of nineteenth- and twentieth-century peoples against the colonial oppressors. As will be seen, the Pueblo Indians made some intelligent and shrewd decisions in their relationship with the Spaniards. On the other hand, the Spaniards were hardly the "fanatically intolerant" masters described by Forbes. Also, it is unrealistic to picture the Pueblo Indians plotting the destruction of their oppressors for eighty years while cynically following the forms of Roman Catholicism and secretly maintaining their old beliefs and practices. The old beliefs were very important, but they were subjected to the syncretism condoned by both the Indian and European.

Scholes's and Forbes's misinterpretations are due in part to problems faced by the Latin American scholar, chief of which is the nature of the documentation. First of all, the sources are sparse, and those that are available are frequently the products of intensely partisan debate — hence rife with charges and countercharges. Such a situation creates source material characterized by pliability and helps to explain how even Scholes and Forbes, advancing two almost diametrically opposed positions, could support their statements with practically the same documentation. One way to correct these misinterpretations is to take a much closer look at the period prior to 1681 and that which followed it. No longer can either period be viewed in isolation since each provides the researcher with clues about the other. This approach yields completely new interpretations of seventeenth-century New Mexican history.

Scholes and Forbes, though opposed in point of view, are essentially alike inasmuch as they describe a society based on relatively simple human relationships. Scholes sees the secular Spaniard fighting the Franciscans for the control of a comparatively mindless mass of Indians. Forbes sees a colonial struggle with the subjected people intent upon throwing off the shackles of Spanish imperialism. Neither simplistic view fits the reality of seventeenth-century New Mexico.

Although it can be said that in this frontier of New Spain both society and government were less formalized than in most other areas of the empire, it does not follow that human and governmental relationships were less complicated. The northernmost province consisted of a variety of distinct aboriginal and nonaboriginal peoples who, in spite of occasional strife, managed to coexist by means of complex accommodations, some of which were even unconscious ones. The associations that the various interest groups had with each other had been established during the eighty years of post-conquest New Mexico — associations which were continually adjusting and often failed to follow the religious or racial patterns described by Scholes and Forbes. Although their interests and even their identities often seem blurred, a number of groups emerge with enough consistency to be differentiated. There were the Athapascan and Pueblo of the aboriginal peoples; among the nonaboriginal population, there were the missionaries, the bureaucratic representatives of Mexico City, the *encomendero,* and the non-*encomendero* members of the Hispanic community.

The Franciscan missionaries quickly established themselves in a position of dominance. These churchmen from the beginning enjoyed advantages which put them in a strategic position for any play in power politics. As Scholes accurately points out:

> All of the clergy were members of Friars Minor. Consequently the church was not weakened by rivalry between various monastic orders or by quarrels between secular and regular clergy. Second, no bishop exercised effective jurisdiction in New Mexico prior to 1680 [or, in fact, for some time thereafter].[12]

The mainstay of Franciscan power, to be sure, rested in the missionaries' relationship with the Indians, a fact which the friars immediately recognized. When, in 1608, it looked as though the Crown might abandon the province, the Franciscans baptized seven thousand Indians within a two-month period in order to force a reversal of the Crown's plans.[13] Within a few years virtually all the Pueblo Indians had been baptized. In those early days the missionaries could hardly be strict about doctrinal matters; the number of conversions was the crucial issue. As Scholes notes: "In the beginning a few elements were stressed such as veneration of the cross, respect for the clergy, instruction concerning the sacraments, the teaching of a few simple prayers, and the regular attendance at religious services."[14] The very incompleteness of so many conversions both required and encouraged considerable latitude and adaptability on the part of Indian and missionary alike: the Indian had to integrate the new teachings into his long-established world view, while the Franciscans had to ignore the hybrid religious forms that inevitably resulted from these rather sudden adjustments.

A typical expression of syncretism is an encounter with the Mansos Indians described by the early chronicler, Fray Alonso de Benavides:

> It was a sight to see those who came on their knees to see the holy cross and to touch and kiss it as they had seen me do. And among others I saw an Indian with a toothache. With great trouble she opened her mouth with her hands and brought her molars close to the holy cross.[15]

The incident clearly demonstrates the syncretism that the meeting of the Old World's Roman Catholic and the North American Indian cultures produced.

Syncretism was hardly a new phenomenon for Spaniards, who did not resist the Mozarabic rite to remain in Toledo. The famous Bishop Juan de Zumarraga had effectively utilized syncretism in central New Spain. In fact, it would be surprising not to find the New Mexican Franciscans utilizing the tradition, since it represented a compromise that was satisfactory for all concerned. On the one hand, it made possible the remarkable incidence of Indian conversions and saved the province for the missionaries; on the other hand, it made acculturation much more tolerable for the Indian.

Even with the advantages, however, the task of limited conversions and acculturation for thousands of Indians in an area extending from Nueva Vizcaya to Taos was a formidable undertaking indeed. To facilitate the inception of this enterprise the Franciscans had to organize the Indian population into rigid and workable entities; the pueblo became the unit of cohesiveness.

Cognizant of political realities, the Franciscans based their rule on a form of directed and controlled self-government. Administrators were first chosen from the Indian leaders, and thereafter an elective method was used. In this manner the missionary bureaucracy was limited in number, and the system, as Bolton observes, "helps to explain how two missionaries and three or four soldiers could make an orderly town out of two or three thousand savages."[16]

With the Indians as a power base, the Franciscans successfully resisted both direct and indirect attacks on their authority. They managed to avoid all attempts at secularization and to elude the authority of the Bishop of Durango. They also resisted most of the frontal attacks launched by the governors.

Contrary to Scholes's thinking, the missionaries had few serious encounters with the *encomendero*. In reality, the missionary and the *encomendero* have much in common. Both had a stake in the survival of the colony, and they depended on each other to maintain it. Both reconciled themselves to a mutual exploitation of the Indian population: the *encomendero* had a degree of military power but lacked legitimate means to keep the often migratory Pueblo from abandoning the *encomienda;* the missionary had the legitimacy but needed the *encomendero*'s power to hold those Indians not coerced by the Franciscan presence. Protection against Athapascan raids was another duty of the *encomendero*. With the reward of souls for the missionary and tribute of maize and cotton *mantas* for the *encomendero,* the two factions entered into a lasting partnership. Even Scholes recognizes their interdependence: "The permanence of the missionaries depended upon the growth of a sizeable nonaboriginal colony."[17] Given the power of the Church in New Mexico, there is little doubt that had the *encomenderos* been at cross purposes with the missionaries, the *encomenderos* would have been eliminated. The seventeenth century offers plenty of examples of the precarious existence of the *encomienda* throughout the empire. The survival of the *encomienda* and the power of the missionary establishment in New Mexico are largely explained by the fact that both factions made pragmatic and durable accommodations.

Scholes is again mistaken when he fails to distinguish the *encomendero* from the governing Spanish bureaucracy.[18] The *encomendero* was usually united with the missionary against the governor and his bureaucracy. Of course there were some antagonisms, especially in the formative period; trouble often erupted when the missionaries moved into new areas already dominated by *encomenderos* though not yet subject to the Church. There were conflicts between overzealous churchmen and equally zealous settlers. Instances of *encomenderos* grumbling about the power of the missionaries and of churchmen complaining about harassment of their charges are by no means fabrications; but these instances were the exceptions and happened in an environment of general accord.

Ironically, Scholes draws attention to cases of common union between missionary and *encomendero* and their mutual antagonism toward the royal government. In the strife between Father Isidro Ordonez and Governor Pedro de Paralta, many of the leading citizens opposed the governor's actions. When Peralta's dissatisfaction with the *encomendero*-Indian relationship led him to interfere, it was Father Ordonez who ordered the governor to cease and desist since the Franciscans were generally satisfied with the *encomenderos'* treatment of the Indians.[19] The satisfaction was largely mutual; for when Peralta finally decided to arrest Father Ordonez, the *encomenderos* abandoned the governor.[20] There are countless other examples of Church-*encomendero* cooperation and their joint opposition to the governing bureaucracy. In 1627 and 1628 Fray Alonso de Benavides received testimony from a group of *encomenderos* charging the governor with heresy, blasphemy, and immorality. Francisco de la Mora Ceballos, governor from 1632 to 1635, also earned the ill-will of both clerical and lay factions, and many of the prominent citizens testified against him.[21]

Governor Luis de Rosas appears on paper to have had a great following and the support of the *cabildo,* but the image is somewhat weakened when one realizes that Rosas controlled the elections that filled the local offices.[22] Of the few *encomenderos* who actually supported him, most held their position only because Rosas had redistributed certain *encomiendas* as spoils.[23] To prove the point, when Rosas left office the *cabildo* elections were held again, and the pro-Rosas nature of the *cabildo* disappeared.[24] By the end of Rosas's term, 73 out of 120 soldiers actively supported the clergy.[25] Rosas was eventually killed with the aid of some highly placed New Mexican citizens; also, and as final proof of cooperation, after the *cabildo* took over control of the government functions, Church-state relations became remarkably smooth.[26]

Furthermore, the governor lacked any real base of power. Whereas the missionary and *encomendero* had the Indian and each other, the governor's power resided in his ability to form usually fragile alliances with disaffected members of the community, to dispense a few fee-paying bureaucratic positions, and to distribute a limited number of *encomiendas*. This diplomacy and patronage, and his prestige as a representative of Mexico City, were the derivations of such power as the governor could muster until 1659 when the power of his office began to increase.

The limited power of the governor brings into question Scholes's interpretation of the governor as an unbridled tyrant. Indeed, even though the missionaries and settlers might have serious differences, they could always rally around one cause: limiting the power of the governor. It is therefore difficult to envisage the plunder ascribed to him by Scholes, who seems a long way from proving his point here. True, the governors were generally profit-oriented; but this merely confirms the nature of Spanish bureaucracy and is hardly a reflection of character. Moreover, in this connection, it should be borne in mind that, in that early period, rarely could economic activities be effectively converted into political power. Missionary and settler each maintained his political and economic prerogatives within the bounds of his own accommodation.

The reason the governors of early New Mexico are interpreted in such negative light is that the documents are strongly biased against them. The explanation should hardly be regarded as strange since the Franciscans' power depended on their ability to neutralize that of the governor, and their most effective way of undermining his power was to produce reams of complaints and attacks. The effects of their *modus operandi* many students of Spanish borderlands tend to underestimate, and Scholes is conspicuously ambivalent in this respect. For instance, he could generalize about the evil character of all governors, yet at the same time he admitted that Governor Peralta (1610–14) was abused by the friars led by Father Ordonez, and he had little criticism of Governor Bernardino de Ceballos, who left office in 1618. Although Governor Juan de Eulate (1618–26) is heavily attacked in *Church and State in New Mexico 1610–1650,* Scholes himself apologizes for the biased nature of his sources. And between 1626 and 1632, Scholes acknowledges there was relative peace.[27]

Even with respect to Governor Francisco de la Mora Ceballos (1632–35), who gave every indication in the literature of being a corrupt tyrant, the documents reveal a pair of noteworthy considerations: (1) his chief accuser was Friar Esteban de Perea, whose antagonism toward all governors was well established; and (2) when Mora returned to Mexico City "he was able to present an adequate justification of his record to the authorities in Mexico City, for he was later appointed commander of the garrison and alcalde mayor of Acapulco."[28] The point here is that it is unrealistic to generalize about the character of the governors since it is impossible to substantiate or refute most of the charges made with the documentation available. What is certain is that the governor often infuriated the clergy, and as a consequence the clergy often exercised all the coercive power at their command to destroy the governors who crossed them. But much is heard about the opposition of the settler group for the obvious reason that they were less prone to fight battles with pen and paper. The absence of documentation cannot justify the conclusion that the settlers supported the governors, as some historians have emphasized. In any event, the existence of a war of words is not conducive to nonbiased documentation.

The independent farmers did not constitute an influential political group during this early period. As the population of New Mexico grew, however, this class of inhabitants gained in relative numbers since the population of other factions was essentially fixed. As shall be pointed out later, the independent farmer was to add a new dimension to New Mexican politics: he furnished a power base for the governors of the later period, and he also complicated relations with the Indian population. With practically no stake in the missionary-*encomendero*-Indian relationship, the farmers contributed to the breakdown of the peace which had been maintained for half a century.

The fact remains that despite occasional small uprisings on the part of the Indians, remarkably stable European-Indian relations prevailed. Such stability was not the product of repression; on the contrary, Spanish-Indian relations grew out of mutual needs. In return for their labor and their souls, the Indians benefited from Spanish military experience, organizational ability, and technology. Much of the aboriginal culture continued — some of it openly, some of it through syncretism, and in still other instances, hidden from view.

Protection against Athapascan raids was an important service performed by the Spaniards. While there is some controversy about the nature of pre-European Athapascan-Pueblo relations,[29] it is known that after the arrival of the European these relations were seriously disrupted. Not only did the Spaniards obtrude themselves between the two Indian groups, they also introduced to the Athapascans the horse as well as a taste for beef. As relations between the two groups worsened, both the striking power of the Athapascan and his perceived need for beef increased. Athapascans began to be seen in a new light even as some of the old trading patterns continued. As Frank Reeve points out, the Apache found it harder and harder to distinguish his Pueblo neighbor from the Spaniard.[30] The Spaniards had early contributed to the deepening gulf between Athapascan and Pueblo; the first governor, Pedro de Peralta, went to New Mexico with orders to keep the Pueblos separated from the surrounding heathens.[31]

As Athapascan raids into Pueblo territory increased, the primary incentive became plunder. Yet Reeve argues that the raids were less economic than political, drawing attention to the number of Pueblo refugees to be found among the Athapascans.[32] The evidence, however, largely substantiates the economic motivation since the Athapascans' raids often meant to them the difference between life and death. As the old trade patterns broke down and the Franciscans gained tighter control over food distribution, Athapascans found friendly barter inadequate. When drought swept New Mexico, conditions became intolerable for all peoples, the bartering relation ended altogether, and the raids became more frequent. Evidence of the latter can be found not only in the dry year of 1641 but also during the disastrous period beginning in 1660.[33] The raids were not without success, as the sources treating 1641 make plain: that year the Pueblos lost 20,000 *fanegas* of maize.[34] The abundance of maize in Pueblo territory must have always been tempting to the Athapascans; but with the coming of the Franciscans, the storing of it became more and more concentrated as well as tempting.

Apart from the drought, the Athapascans' normal channels of trade began to be obstructed in more effective ways, especially after 1660.[35] As events progressed, the Pueblo Indian came to rely on the organizing talent of the European. The Indian was impressed, of course, by the efficiency with which this talent expressed itself in weaponry and military strategy. Since the Spaniards controlled defense, the Pueblos depended upon them for protection not only against the plundering Athapascans but from each other as well.

The Spanish talent for organization expressed itself in other ways. It brought a degree of prosperity to the Pueblo Indians. Spanish crops supplemented those cultivated by the Indian, and more importantly, new methods of storing food through the winter greatly aided in preventing starvation in the harsh New Mexican climate. It is well known that after the poor harvest of the late 1660s, the missionaries saved many Indians from starvation.[36]

Needless to say, the Spaniard's ability to organize gave him military advantage vis-à-vis the Pueblo. Spanish unity was maintained while the interpueblo animosity was fostered. The entire pre-1670 period abounds with instances of the governor of one pueblo informing on conspirators in others. For example, Indian revolts in 1645 and 1650 were put down as a result of information supplied by other Indians. As long as the Spaniards could obtain such intelligence and punish the offenders with little worry about a response from other pueblos, their military superiority was assured.

Thus, along with compromise, toleration, and a few real benefits, fear of military reprisal did much to keep the peace among the Pueblo Indians. As Fray Alonso de Benavides wrote:

> Though few and ill-equipped, God has assured that the Spaniard always come out victorious and has instilled in the Indian such a fear of the Spanish and their arquebuses that if he hears that a Spaniard is coming to his pueblo he flees.[37]

This fear was certainly instrumental in inducing the Indians to submit not only to the missionary fathers but also, at times, to abusive Europeans. Such military superiority could be maintained only as long as the environment of the Pueblo Indian was tolerable enough to allow interpueblo animosity to take precedence over anti-Spanish feeling.

Such a state of affairs significantly altered New Mexican politics from what could have been expected had Santa Fe been closer to the seats of

power. Military might had its limitations in so remote an area, and the policies of a generally intolerant Europe had to be compromised by the realities of the frontier. It must be remembered that most of the relationships
between non-Indian groups were primarily shaped by the need to stabilize
relations with the Indians. Hence, quite contrary to what might be expected
from seventeenth-century Europeans, there developed in New Mexico a degree of tolerance and many mutually advantageous accommodations — all
of which was first of all imperative for the survival of the European colony,
and incidentally afforded to the Pueblo Indians, at least temporarily, a feeling of security, well-being, and peace. While holding no promise as a
panacea for the problems of either race, it proved to be a fairly stable
arrangement for a colonial frontier society since it lasted for nearly three-
quarters of a century.

But in the 1670s the Spanish-Indian relationship fell apart, and the reason for its disintegration was that the Indian ceased to be a willing partner.
His resistance grew and culminated in the Pueblo Revolt of 1680. With the
Indian now withdrawn from the social, economic, and political life within
the province, the Europeans were compelled to adjust to the reality of a
drastically changed situation.

Just why the Revolt occurred is the subject of much speculation. Scholes,
leading one school of interpretation, saw the Revolt as the outcome of the
church-state strife. He believed that the Indians became so demoralized by
the irresponsible actions of the Hispanic settlers and their interminable
feuding that the Pueblos decided to take matters into their own hands. John
Francis Bannon is clearly a contemporary proponent of this school.[38] On
the other hand, Charles Wilson Hackett saw the Revolt as the inevitable
consequence of the century-long struggle of the Spaniards to suppress the
religious beliefs, habits, and customs of the Pueblo. According to Hackett,
the aggressive proselytism generated frictions which finally exploded in
1680.[39] Jack Forbes saw the Revolt as a result of not only long-term religious
persecution but also racial and economic abuses. All three factors impelled
the Indians to plot and overthrow the imperialist.[40]

Interpretations premised on a continuum of abuses have one basic fault:
they assume that some sort of dialectic was operating — which clearly was
not always the case in New Mexico. These widely accepted analyses of the
outbreak derive mainly from a general misunderstanding of seventeenth-
century New Mexican history and, in particular, of the documentary evidence concerning the Pueblo Revolt itself. For instance, fear and misinfor-
mation, growing out of faulty intelligence, induced the Spaniards to point
to the religious character of the rebellion. As a result, modern historians
have emphasized this facet far out of proportion to its actual relevance.[41]

Even more fundamentally, however, most of the interpretations are the
products of a serious misunderstanding of the nature of human relations in

seventeenth-century New Mexico. The causes and the nature of the Revolt grew out of these relations, which had themselves by that time grown both complex and precarious. What indeed happened was that the whole system of interaction weakened during the 1670s, and the progression of events culminated in the final break of 1680. The Spaniards had begun to fail in their part of the system; put simply, collaboration ceased to be profitable for the Pueblo Indian.

The chief impetus arose out of the problems created by the prolonged drought of the late 1660s and the great famines that followed it in the 1670s. The kind of peace that had been pervading New Mexico was contingent upon relative prosperity. Spanish improvements in food production, storage, and distribution had helped to create the surpluses needed to support the colony. The famine of 1670, however, was so severe that it set in motion the process which led to the complete collapse of the system.

As already noted, the missionaries did supply food to the Indians in the latter part of the 1660s; but the drought persisted, and the suffering it caused cannot be overstated. As Fray Francisco de Ayeta later wrote to the King:

> In the year 1670 there was great famine in these provinces which compelled the Spanish inhabitants and Indians alike to eat hides and straps of the carts. . . . There followed in the next year a great pestilence which carried off many people and cattle. . . .[42]

As it became apparent that the Spaniards could no longer ward off the natural disasters of drought and famine, the foreign settlers' control over the stores of food which still remained must have become conspicuously oppressive to the indigenous peoples.

Another effect of the famine of 1670 was the intensification of Athapascan raids. The drought undoubtedly forced the now mobile Athapascan from the mountains in search of sustenance. As Ayeta also wrote to the King:

> Apaches who were then at peace rebelled and rose up, and the said province was totally sacked and robbed by their attacks and outraged. . . . It is common knowledge that from the year 1672 until your excellency adopted measures for aiding the kingdom six pueblos were depopulated.[43]

Unrest mounted and Spanish soldiers began to suffer severe setbacks as their arms proved ineffective against the Athapascan onslaught.

Not only were the Athapascans humbling Spanish power, but the Pueblo Indians were contributing to its humiliation as well. In 1675, for instance, when Juan Trevino was governor, a group of Indians was arrested on charges of bewitching the Padre Andres Duran. Four who admitted to the witchcraft were hanged; the others were sentenced to be lashed or imprisoned. As the prisoners were awaiting the implementation of justice, a telling event occurred. A group of Indian warriors entered the governor's house with the dual purpose of killing Trevino and rescuing the condemned Indians. To save his own life, the governor freed the prisoners,[44] and the Spanish military proved itself incapable of any sort of quick response to their fury. The mere loss of prestige itself had a devastating effect upon the now alarmingly outnumbered Spaniards, for the Indians were no longer to be intimidated as they had been since early in the century.

Also relevant here is the cause of the daring incident of 1675. Strong reaction against Indian ways had been developing among segments of the Hispanic community. In the 1660s, for instance, Governor Lopez de Mendizabal was forced to resist efforts on the part of the Church and some settlers to crack down on Pueblo religious and cultural activity.[45] It was the growth of such nativism that had led to the Trevino episode.

The reason for the movement toward nativism is open to speculation, but the growing number of mestizos may have had something to do with it. It could well have been that Indian culture was spreading through the population of mixed-bloods and thus receiving too much attention in the European colony. While syncretism was tolerated from the Indian community, when it began to show signs of diffusion throughout the Spanish colony, some sort of reaction was to be expected. If such were in fact the case, one could predict that the mestizo would play a confused role in the Revolt; and so he did, for during and after the rebellion mixed-bloods could be found fighting on both sides — hence against each other.

The tensions of the 1670s caused Spanish hostility to surface more flagrantly. As the Europeans' condonation of syncretism began to fade, the very foundation for Indian tolerance of Spanish rule began to disappear too.[46] The reactionary attitude of their Spanish rulers became at once a threat to the fundamental nature of Indian culture and a source of frustration to mestizos who had found identification in both worlds. A counter nativistic movement was indeed a more than likely response.

Certainly there was no lack of leadership for such a movement. Benavides quoted a shaman as once having screamed:

> You Spaniards and Christians, how crazy you are! And you live like crazy folks! You want to teach us to be crazy also. . . . You Christians are so crazy that you go all together flogging yourselves like crazy people in the streets, shedding your blood. And thus you wish that the Pueblo be also crazy.[47]

Pueblos of this mind were probably active in many of the earlier aborted revolts, such as that of 1645 which resulted in the execution of forty Indians, or the one in 1659 in which nine Indians were executed and many en-slaved.[48] Yet those earlier revolts were sporadic and involved little inter-pueblo cooperation.

But the fact that this caliber of leadership had not been at all uncommon theretofore among the Pueblos raises a question as to how strategic was the contribution of the famous Popé in fomenting the final Revolt of 1680. Al-though in the documents he is consistently referred to as its prime instiga-tor, there is little evidence marking Popé as a unique Indian leader beyond the fact that the Revolt of 1680 was a success. He was a shaman and had been arrested in 1675 for that very reason. The 1670s had simply presented that set of conditions in which this kind of leadership could be effectual. To-gether, the disappearance of the positive attitudes and elements of Spanish rule and the growth of Spanish nativism understandably encouraged both disaffection and nativism among the Indians themselves. Much of the mis-interpretation of the Revolt of 1680 can be attributed to an overemphasis on the contribution of this one man and singling out his conspiracy as the cause of the Revolt.[49]

Actually, the one-time collaborators had now become resistors and for crucial reasons. When Popé issued his call to arms, he was merely echoing the feeling of most of the people. The harsh conditions of existence of the 1670s together with the Spaniards' move toward nativism, demonstrated by their developing religious and cultural intolerance, made it plain that In-dian culture, well-being, and even survival were in jeopardy. Somewhat ironically, the program which Popé offered to his people was in many ways similar to that offered them by the Spaniards in the past. The revival of In-dian culture which he championed was mostly symbolic in nature and a re-action to those facets of the Spanish culture which either had failed or were most threatening the cultural existence of the Pueblo.

Paradoxically, it was acculturation which had in the long run made the Revolt of 1680 possible. In the years of contact with the European, the In-dian's technological disadvantage in warfare had been appreciably nar-rowed. The *cabildo* of Santa Fe described the Indians of this time as "good horsemen and as experienced as any Spaniard in the use of firearms, [and] well acquainted with the entire territory of New Mexico."[50]

Even apart from religious conflict, the Church was the focal point of Spanish-Indian contact and consequently received the brunt of the Revolt. The relationship between the Church and the Revolt has been another source of misinterpretation. In examining this problem two questions must be asked: (1) what aspects of church life were rejected by the Indians? and (2) did their rejections represent a drive for religious freedom, or were they a thrust against a secular force?

Superficially the Revolt appears to have been an outright repudiation of Roman Catholicism. Twenty-one fathers out of thirty-two were killed, and the missions, when not destroyed, were defiled. Popé traveled from pueblo to pueblo demanding that his people burn the images, temples, rosaries, and crosses. He told them to forsake the names given them in holy baptism and advised the men to leave the women given them in holy matrimony. They were forbidden to mention the name of God, of the Blessed Virgin, and names of the saints or the Blessed Sacrament. He further ordered them to wash themselves with amole root in order to free themselves from the condition of holy baptism.[51]

On closer examination, however, one can see that Popé used syncretism to his own advantage in much the same way as the Spaniards had been doing since the beginning of the century. By 1680 many European concepts had been adapted to Pueblo world views, and Popé was utilizing these syncretic expressions along with the concepts of pre-European origin. For instance, he claimed to have contact with three gods, and one of them, "father of all Indians, who had been so since the flood," had ordered him to tell the Indians to rebel.[52] Popé also claimed direct contact with the devil who he now argued was much stronger than the Christian God.[53] Both claims were said to have instilled deep fear in the natives. The conclusion is inescapable: instead of repudiating Christian concepts and legend, Popé often tailored them to fit the new need. In this way, syncretism became a cornerstone of the revolution.

The Indians' fear of military reprisals, something the Spanish could no longer count on, became another element of Popé's strategy. He exploited it in order to develop the necessary adherence to the conspiracy and to insure secrecy as well as cohesiveness. It was common knowledge among the Indians that Popé had murdered his son-in-law in the belief that his own daughter's husband was a security leak.[54] Popé also let it be known that those pueblos which refused to join in the Revolt would be destroyed and all their inhabitants with them.[55]

But while fear was a real factor in effecting compliance, Popé's leadership made a positive appeal to the native population and won their loyalty largely because the time was ripe. When captive Indians were interrogated by Otermín in 1681, they reaffirmed their determination to fight the Spaniards to the death if necessary in order to preserve their way of life.[56]

One of the positive elements in Popé's movement was his promise to end the incursions of the Athapascans. This objective, to be accomplished through a series of Pueblo-Athapascan alliances,[57] was a crucial one for the relatively sedentary people whose immobility dangerously exposed them to attack. While these alliances did not eliminate the Pueblos' vulnerability altogether, the small number of complaints registered in Otermín's inquest of 1681 amply demonstrates that the situation had vastly improved over what it had been under Spanish rule.

The great famines of the 1670s, as noted earlier, were a critical factor in generating a mood of rebellion among the Indian population. Although Popé failed to solve the problem, he unified and encouraged his people and incited them to action by means of grandiose promises of future prosperity. He pledged that,

> by living under the laws of their ancients, they would raise a great quantity of corn and beans, large bolls of cotton, pumpkins and watermelons of great size and musk melons, and that their houses would be filled and they would have good health and plenty of rest.[58]

Thus Popé became to his own people an acceptable alternative to the Spaniards. Not only did he promise to restore to them all that they had had prior to 1670, he also offered them an opportunity to preserve their cultural identity, the survival of which Spanish reactionary policies were then threatening. As such an alternative, however, he would be subjected to the same forces as the governors of New Mexico had been. Another famine hit the area, and the recultivated Athapascan friendship vanished.[59] Popé's cultural program eventually got out of hand when he went so far as to prohibit the planting of all seeds save the traditional ones, corn and beans.[60] The original leader of the Revolt of 1680 soon fell from power. Popé, however, was not the revolution, for it persevered under new leadership. The movement was neither the expression of nor dependent on one sagacious Indian; rather, it was the consequence of the collapse of a long series of delicately balanced human relationships between foreign settlers and indigenous peoples. Popé was there to personify aboriginal frustration and antagonism.

Since the very existence of the province throughout its entire history depended upon Spanish-Indian relations, when these were disrupted, the fabric of Spanish society convulsed. Realignments of its several factions followed; in addition, there were signs of a class struggle with many mestizos and mulattoes aligning with the Indians against the Europeans and those aboriginal collaborators who had remained loyal. With total disruption of the balances that had enabled the Spaniards to rule, and with the Indians approaching technological equality in warfare, revolution had become almost inevitable.

The plan for the Revolt was tactically superb. Secrecy had been strictly maintained, and the plans had been quietly distributed among the leaders of all the pueblos — excepting that of the Piros who were not to be trusted. Knotted cords were left with each of the leaders; when the pueblos had agreed to the plans for a revolt on August 13, 1680, their leaders began untying the knots. Once the Revolt was started, the goal was complete annihilation of the foreigners. The Indians planned to regroup after the fall of

Santa Fe and proceed south to ambush the fleeing survivors.[61] Although not all the plans of the Pueblos came to fruition, the Revolt was well executed.

The situation in colonial New Mexico had been precarious for some time. In the years preceding the Revolt, conditions had worsened to the degree that Fray Ayeta had been ordered south to garner aid from the viceregal officials. He left Mexico City on February 27, 1677, with fifty convict soldiers and arrived at Santa Fe nine months later with 44,[62] six of the men having deserted en route; the rest, excepting three volunteers, would likely have fled had they not been chained to their saddles. Ayeta reported to the King on May 10, 1679, that as a result of the action taken, "the nascent spark did not become a conflagration to burn and lay waste these provinces,"[63] but that the situation was extremely insecure, and he asked the King for more men and a presidio for Santa Fe.[64]

The population figures alone are revealing. J. Manuel Espinosa estimates the entire Spanish population of New Mexico at the time as being not more than 2,800 with the Christianized Pueblo Indians numbering 35,000.[65] The Indian population is a matter of conjecture, however, and Espinosa's judgment seems to be exaggerated. Ayeta, basing his figures on church records, placed the number of Christianized Pueblo Indians at about 16,000.[66] An estimate from the *cabildo* of Santa Fe put the number at 17,000,[67] and since the *cabildo* was trying at this time to emphasize the strength of the revolutionary Indians, it would be unlikely that it would underestimate their number. Hence a figure between 16,000 and 17,000 would seem reasonable. Ayeta believed that 6,000 of these were capable of bearing arms. It is significant that Ayeta was counting the Pueblo Indians as part of the Spanish forces, and while stressing the scarcity of Spanish fighting men,[68] it would have been out of order for Ayeta to overestimate the size of the Indian forces. These figures do not include the heathen Athapascans, who were temporarily aiding the Pueblo Indians during the insurrection and increasing their numbers markedly.

Ayeta concluded that the number of Spaniards who could bear arms was approximately 170, including the 44 he had brought up from Mexico City,[69] and added that not more than 20 Spaniards could be assembled at one time or place. At this time there were 32 missionaries among the pueblos, 21 of whom were later to be killed outright.[70] After the Revolt, the viceroy reported to the King that of the Spaniards, 380 had been killed, "not sparing the defenseless, of the women and children."[71] The *cabildo* reported the same figure, adding that among those lost were 73 men capable of carrying arms. Using Ayeta's and the *cabildo*'s numbers, about 100 men were left who were capable of bearing arms,[72] an estimate that is close to Governor Otermín's muster after the Revolt.[73] Excluding the Apache allies, the ratio of revolting Indian warriors to fighting Spaniards was 60:1. Indians were no longer the acquiescent and defenseless souls of Benavides' day; now they were natives who had reached a high degree of acculturation in their three-quarters of a century of contact with the Spaniards.

The exact date on which the Revolt started is uncertain. According to a letter from Fray Ayeta to Otermín, it was August 10, 1680.[74] There is much evidence, however, that although it was scheduled for August 13, the Revolt began on August 9, the date fixed by the *cabildo* of Santa Fe in a letter to the governor[75] and based on reports from the Spaniards, Fray Juan Bernal, Fray Fernando de Valasco, and Captain Mario de Dehenzas.[76] On the same day, the governors of Tanos and Pecos issued a warning of impending revolt,[77] and these warnings were justified by intelligence gained from two captured Indian conspirators. On the next day reports of death in the hinterland began to filter into the villa, one of which came from a Pedro Hidalgo who reported the death of one Cristobal de Herrera on the previous day.[78] Some hostilities apparently did break out on August 9.

Although Otermín at first failed to grasp the seriousness of the situation, he was quick to admit his blunder and then lost no time in establishing a defense around Santa Fe. He organized this defense none too soon, for the Revolt quickly made its way to the doors of Santa Fe.[79] After a siege, described as having lasted either seven or nine days, the settlers petitioned the governor for an immediate retreat, and he agreed.[80] By this time there was hardly an alternative, for much of the villa had already been burned and the water supply cut off. With over a thousand persons huddled in the buildings still standing, the Spanish position was hopeless.[81] Provisions were so low that, as Otermín was later to write of the evacuation,

> I trusted divine providence, for I left without a crust of bread or grain of wheat or maize, and with no other provision for the convoy of so many people except four hundred animals and two carts belonging to private persons, and for food, a few sheep, goats, and cows.[82]

The plan called for supplying at Isleta, but this was impossible since Isleta had been abandoned before the refugees reached it. Over a month passed before the refugees obtained provisions other than those gleaned from the land or bought or stolen from the Indians.

While Governor Otermín and the other refugees were fighting for their survival as they continued south, the atmosphere in the El Paso district had become one of great confusion and wild speculation. Reports of revolt had been seeping in, and the belief was that all whites north of Isleta had been slaughtered, yet nothing was certain.[83] Although in late August aid had been sent north to the settlers who had abandoned Isleta, it was not until September 4 that it was learned that the Governor was still alive and leading the refugees south.[84]

Otermín soon united the Isleta and Santa Fe refugees into one settlement. But conditions were so miserable that despite even the use of force to hold the people together, desertion from the new settlement became a major problem. When the Governor concluded count on February 8, 1681, he still had 1,946 under his command. Of these only 150 could bear arms, and he counted only 171 horses and mules. The scarcity of fighting men, low state of his supplies, and the advice of his officers led Otermín to delay the reconquest.[85] At this moment, Spanish New Mexico was at the crossroads of its history.

Notes

1. The main thrust of my research has been in the period following the Pueblo Revolt of 1680, my interest being the economic, social, and political changes that occurred in El Paso as a result of the dislocations caused by the Revolt. (See an article to be published in the *Journal of the West*, "The Dynamics of Change: New Mexico 1680 to 1690.") The analysis of the data I collected clearly pointed to relationships that had not been described by experts on the period before the Pueblo Revolt. A desire to understand the inconsistency led me to examine the literature a little more closely and critically, and I found certain mistakes of evidence and logic that, unless they are understood, confuse the rest of New Mexican history. In this reexamination I never had any intention of re-researching or rewriting pre–Pueblo Revolt New Mexican history. I only intended to propose a plausible alternative which would be compatible with what I knew to be the case in the period following the Revolt.

2. France V. Scholes, *Church and State in New Mexico 1610–1650* (Albuquerque, 1937), p. 192.

3. France V. Scholes, *Troublous Times in New Mexico, 1659–1670* (Albuquerque, 1942), p. 29.

4. Scholes, *Church and State*, p. 15.

5. Scholes, *Troublous Times*, pp. 7–8.

6. Ibid., p. 255.

7. Ibid., p. 116.

8. Scholes, *Church and State*, p. 195.

9. Since Scholes wrote a number of articles before publishing these two books, most of the same ideas are found in the articles which include "Church and State in New Mexico, 1610–1650," *New Mexico Historical Review*, XI (Jan., Apr., July, Oct., 1936), 12 (Jan., 1937); "Problems in the Early Ecclesiastical History of New Mexico," *New Mexico Historical Review*, 7 (Jan., 1932); "The First Decade of the Inquisition in New Mexico," *New Mexico Historical Review*, 10 (July, 1935); "Troublous Times in New Mexico, 1659–1670," *New Mexico Historical Review*, 12 (Apr., Oct., 1937), 13 (Jan., 1938), 15 (July, Oct., 1940), 16 (Jan., Apr., July, 1941); "Civil Government and Society in New Mexico in the 17th Century," *New Mexico Historical Review*, 10 (Jan., 1935); "The Supply Service of the New Mexico Missions," *New Mexico Historical Review*, 5 (Jan., Apr., Oct., 1930).

10. Jack D. Forbes, *Apache, Navaho, and Spaniard* (Oklahoma, 1960), p. 177.

11. Ibid., pp. 185–86.

12. Scholes, *Church and State*, p. 16.

13. Forbes, *Apache, Navaho, and Spaniard*, p. 112.

14. Scholes, *Church and State*, p. 13.

15. Fray Alonso de Benavides, *The Memorial of Fray Alonso de Benevides*, 1630, trans. by Mrs. Edward E. Ayer (Albuquerque, 1965), p. 15. I have improved the translation. The Mansos were an Athapascan speaking people located in the general El Paso area.

16. Herbert E. Bolton, "The Mission as a Frontier Institution in the Spanish American Colonies," *American Historical Review*, 23 (Oct., 1917), 61.

17. Scholes, *Church and State*, p. 89.

18. Ibid. Scholes's concept of history seems flexible, since he can and does differentiate at times.

19. Ibid., p. 140. Contrary to the general picture painted by Scholes, it was Peralta who complained about the *encomenderos'* relationship with the Indian. Scholes incorrectly tries to argue that Ordonez was the one who opposed the *encomenderos'* treatment of the Indians but tricked Peralta into bringing the cases against the settlers. Certainly there was conflict between Ordonez and the settlers, but the extent of it is impossible to assess. The fact remains that when facing the governor, Ordonez was backed by the settlers.

20. Ibid., pp. 32, 43, 71, 78, 81. In a weak attempt to substantiate the split between settler and missionary, Scholes gives the example of Alferez Juan Escarrmad who was attacked by the Church. Such an example, however, confuses the issue for Escarrmad was one of the few settlers who actually supported Peralta (p. 43). Scholes uses misleading examples throughout his book. He cites citizens who allegedly supported the Governor, extracting their names from caustic documents written by the missionaries who were at the time attacking many prominent people. These acidic remarks grew out of a temporary dispute over collection of tribute that ended in 1621 (p. 78). As a matter of fact, the governor had to issue orders forcing the citizens to stop aiding the missionaries (p. 71). Actually, Scholes fails to provide much evidence to support his contentions that the settlers were at loggerheads with the Church and that they mercilessly exploited the Indian (p. 89).

21. See ibid., pp. 103, 104, 111–12, for examples.

22. Ibid., p. 154.

23. Ibid., p. 150.

24. Ibid., p. 154. Scholes's interpretation is that the anti-Rosas faction was gaining control; actually, it appears that the settler representation was simply returning to normal.

25. Ibid., p. 165, n.

26. Ibid., pp. 155, 174–75.

27. Ibid., pp. 103–04.

28. Ibid., p. 106.

29. Forbes argues convincingly that Athapascan-Pueblo relations were friendly before the arrival of the Spaniards. Unfortunately, he fails to argue convincingly that the amicable relations continued after the Europeans' arrival.

30. Frank Reeve, "Seventeenth Century Navaho-Spanish Relations," *New Mexico Historical Review*, 31 (Jan., 1957), 42.

31. Forbes, *Apache, Navaho, and Spaniard*, pp. 111–12.

32. Reeve argues that the pueblos were heavily fortified, poorly provisioned, and

willing to trade, and if supplies were desired the Athapascans could easily have traded for them.

33. Scholes, *Troublous Times,* p. 253, and *Church and State,* p. 142. Scholes cites these examples, though, he sees the Apache raids not as a search for food but as a military move which takes advantage of Pueblo and Spanish disarray and misery.

34. Scholes, *Church and State,* p. 142, countering the argument that the Pueblos were so poor that raids would not have been profitable.

35. Reeve, "Seventeenth Century Navaho-Spanish Relations," p. 48.

36. Letter from Fray Francisco de Ayeta to the King, May 10, 1679, in Charles Wilson Hackett, *Historical Documents Relating to New Mexico, Nueva Vizcaya and Approaches Thereto to 1773,* 3 vols. (Washington, 1937), 3:298–302 (cited hereafter as Hackett, *Documents*).

37. Benavides, *Memorial,* pp. 56–57.

38. John Francis Bannon, *The Spanish Borderlands Frontier 1513–1821* (New York, 1970), p. 80.

39. Charles Wilson Hackett, ed., *Revolt of the Pueblo Indians of New Mexico and Otermín's Attempted Reconquest, 1680–1682* (Albuquerque, 1942), 1:xxii–xxiii.

40. Forbes, *Apache, Navaho, and Spaniard,* p. 177.

41. Ibid.

42. Letter from Fray Francisco de Ayeta to the King, May 10, 1679, in Hackett, *Documents,* 3:302.

43. Ibid., pp. 298–302.

44. Declarations of Luis de Quintana, Diego Lopez Sambrano, and Fray Francisco de Ayeta, Dec. 22–23, 1681, in Hackett, *Revolt,* II, 289, 300, 309.

45. Scholes, *Troublous Times,* pp. 61, 98.

46. Spanish reaction often took the form of abuse. Much Indian resentment was leveled at Secretary Francisco Xavier, *Maestre de Campo* Alonso Garcia, and *Sargentos Mayores* Don Luis de Quintana and Diego Lopez, all of whom were accused of administering beatings, subjecting the Indians to forced labor and taking their belongings. From the interrogation of an Indian, Jose, on Dec. 19, 1681, by Otermín, and from his interrogation of two other Indians, Juan Lorenzo and Francisco Lorenzo, Dec. 20, 1681, in Ralph E. Twitchell, *The Spanish Archives of New Mexico* (Cedar Rapids, Iowa, 1914), 2:57 and 66, respectively (cited hereafter as Twitchell, *Archives*).

47. Benavides, *Memorial,* pp. 20–21.

48. Interview with Diego Lopez Sambrano, Dec. 22, 1681, in Hackett, *Revolt,* 2:298–299.

49. Fray Angelico Chavez' work, "Pohé-yemo's Representative and the Pueblo Revolt of 1680," *New Mexico Historical Review,* 42 (Jan., 1967), carries this idea to the extreme by concluding that the Indians were incited to revolt by a black man.

50. Letter from the *cabildo* of Santa Fe to Otermín, Oct. 3, 1680, in Twitchell, *Archives,* 2:53.

51. Letter written by the *cabildo* of Santa Fe, Oct. 3, 1680, in Twitchell, *Archives,* 2:49; a list of the 21 missionaries is found in Hackett, *Documents,* 3:336–39.

52. Interviews with various Indians in ibid., pp. 52, 64.

53. Interrogation of Diego Lopez Sambrano, in Hackett, *Revolt,* 2:295.

54. Interrogation of an Indian, Juan, Dec. 28, 1681, in Twitchell, *Archives,* 2:52–53.

55. Ibid., p. 53.

56. Auto by Otermín, Aug. 9, 1680, in Hackett, *Revolt,* 1:5; taken from an interview with an Indian, Aug, 25, 1680, by Otermín, in Twitchell, *Archives,* 2:18.

57. Various interrogations of Indians in Twitchell, *Archives,* 2:57–67.

58. Auto of Otermín, Sept. 8, 1680, in Hackett, *Documents,* 3:335.

59. Interrogation of an Indian, Lucas, by Otermin, Dec. 18, 1681, in Twitchell, *Archives,* 2:64.

60. Ralph E. Twitchell, *The Leading Facts of New Mexico History* (Cedar Rapids, Iowa, 1911), p. 369.

61. Interrogation of an Indian, Juan, by Otermín, Dec. 28, 1681, in Twitchell, *Archives,* 2:53.

62. Interrogation of an Indian, Antonio, by Otermín, Aug. 23, 1680, in ibid., p. 14.

63. Letter from Fray Francisco de Ayeta to the King, May 10, 1679, in Hackett, *Documents,* 3:298.

64. Ibid., p. 299.

65. Letter from Francisco de Montago, Feb. 27, 1677, attesting to the fact that 47 convicts and 3 volunteers went with Fray Ayeta, in Hackett, *Documents,* 3:316.

66. J. Manuel Espinosa, *Crusaders of the Rio Grande* (Chicago, 1942), pp. 16, 19.

67. Letter from Fray Francisco de Ayeta to the King, May 10, 1679, in Hackett, *Documents,* 3:298–99.

68. Letter written by the *cabildo* of Santa Fe, Oct. 3, 1680, in Twitchell, *Archives,* 2:46.

69. Letter from Fray Francisco de Ayeta to the King, May 10, 1679, in Hackett, *Documents,* 3:298–99.

70. Ibid.

71. Report of the viceroy to the King, Feb. 28, 1681, in Hackett, *Documents,* 3:339.

72. Letter written by the *cabildo* of Santa Fe, Oct. 3, 1680, in Twitchell, *Archives,* 2:44.

73. Petition by the *cabildo* of Santa Fe to Otermín, Sept. 1680, in Twitchell, *Archives,* 2:39; the muster held by Otermín, Feb. 8, 1681, in Hackett, *Documents,* 3:342.

74. Letter from Otermín to Fray Francisco de Ayeta, Sept. 8, 1680, in Hackett, *Documents,* 3:336.

75. Letter written by the *cabildo* of Santa Fe, Oct. 3, 1680, in Twitchell, *Archives,* 2:43.

76. Auto by Otermín, Aug. 9, 1680, in Hackett, *Revolt,* 1:3.

77. Letter from Otermín to Fray Francisco de Ayeta, Sept. 8, 1680, in Hackett, *Documents,* 2:328.

78. The first Auto of Otermín, Aug. 9, 1680, in Hackett, *Revolt,* I. 7.

79. Second Auto of Otermín, Aug. 9, 1680; judicial process and declaration, Aug. 10, 1680; Declaration of *Maestre de Campo* Francisco Gomez, Aug. 14, 1680; Auto of Otermín, Aug. 13, 1680; letter from Otermín to viceroy, Oct. 20, 1680; all in Hackett, *Revolt,* 1:7–11, 208.

80. From Otermín come two sources of information about the assault on Santa Fe; both contain discrepancies. According to a letter from Otermín to Fray Ayeta, the assault began on Aug. 13 and continued until the retreat to Isleta on the following Monday, Aug. 19, implying a siege of only seven days (Hackett, *Documents,* 3:330–34). According to Autos of Otermín, the attack began on Aug. 15 with the retreat commencing on the 21st, again only a seven-day siege (Hackett, *Revolt,*

1:13–19). Both sources, however, refer to a nine-day siege. It is conceivable that Otermín, when referring to a nine-day assault in the Autos, meant to begin the battle on Aug. 13, the day he ordered the fortification of Santa Fe. This would explain the nine-day Indian offensive. The Autos were a day-by-day account of the events and are bound to be more accurate. The letter to Ayeta, although cited by many authorities, cannot be regarded as accurate on this point; it was written amid great hardship almost a month after the fact, and contained no internal evidence to explain Otermín's mention of a nine-day assault on the villa. This discrepancy should not invalidate the letter as a good source of information.

81. Letter from Otermín to Fray Francisco de Ayeta, Sept. 8, 1680, in Hackett, *Documents,* 3:332; Auto of Otermín, Aug. 13–20, 1680, in Hackett, *Revolt,* 1:15.

82. Letter from Otermín to Fray Francisco de Ayeta, Sept. 8, 1680, in Hackett, *Documents,* 3:334.

83. Auto of the *Junta,* Aug. 25, 1680, in Hackett, *Revolt,* 1:32.

84. Letter from *Maestre de Campo* Alonso Garcia to *Maestre de Campo* Leira, Sept. 4, 1680, in Hackett, *Revolt,* 1:54–55.

85. Hackett, *Documents,* 3:342.

4. Did the right leader make the revolt possible?

Angélico Chávez

Pohé-yemo's Representative and the Pueblo Revolt of 1680

Born in New Mexico in 1910, Angélico Chávez entered a Franciscan seminary in 1924, inspired by what he had read about the achievements of Franciscans in the missions of California and New Mexico. He died in 1996 after a long career as a priest in his native New Mexico and as one of his native state's most prolific and revered writers of history, poetry, and fiction.

The strong influences of Chávez's Catholic-Hispanic back-ground seem clear in this article, "Pohé-yemo's Represen-tatives and the Pueblo Revolt of 1680," which appeared in the *New Mexico Historical Review* in 1967. Unlike Bowden and Gutiérrez, who see deep religious differences as a funda-mental cause of the Pueblo Revolt, Chávez suggests that tolerant Franciscans gave the Pueblos no cause for revolt. Pueblo leaders claimed religious persecution as a pretext to gain "power and revenge." And those Pueblo leaders, he concludes, were *mestizos* (or *coyotes* as they were also called in New Mexico) rather than pure-blooded Pueblos.

Some of Chávez's analysis seems wrong-headed by today's standards. He confuses race with culture and attributes in-herent characteristics to entire peoples. To him, Pueblos were a "peaceful people," Apaches were "warlike," and mu-lattoes like Domingo Naranjo were "more active and rest-less by nature than the more passive and stolid Indian." Pueblo religion, which he called "mythology," had "no Cre-ation Myth," and Pueblos worshiped no "god," but rather a "Power." His judgments about entire peoples and his dismissal of Pueblo religion reveal more about Chávez's mind than about his subject. They should not, however, diminish our appreciation of his imaginative detective work, which allows him to read familiar sources in new ways.

Chávez identifies one mixed-blood leader in particular, Domingo Naranjo, as the leader of the Pueblo Revolt. Described to Spaniards by Pueblo informants as a tall, black man with yellow eyes, Domingo Naranjo had posed as a representative from the god Pohé-yemo, directed operations from a *kiva* in Taos during the revolt, and successfully concealed his identity from Spaniards both during and after the revolt. Drawing from his deep knowledge of the genealogies of early Spanish families in New Mexico (he wrote the definitive book on the subject), Chávez elaborates on five generations of Naranjos. The reader can easily get lost in the details of Part 2 of this essay, but historical work can be as technical as that of any other field and Chávez needs to present and interpret the evidence to make his complicated case. Out of that evidence comes his conclusion that Domingo Naranjo, a man who lived as a Pueblo Indian at the Tewa-speaking pueblo of Santa Clara, was actually the descendent of a black man who understood much about the beliefs of Indians in central Mexico as well as about Pueblo and Spanish ways and so successfully led the revolt in the guise of a representative of the god Pohé-yemo.

Perhaps because he bases this argument on "mere reasoned conjecture" and it cannot be proved or disproved, most students of the Pueblo Revolt have neither dismissed it nor accepted it. Some simply ignore it; others bury it in their notes, as did Bowden and Garner. In the only detailed consideration of Chávez's position, historian Stefanie Beninato agreed with him that a mulatto named Naranjo played a key role by posing as Pohé-yemo but disagreed that he was the principal leader. Instead, she saw this Naranjo as one of several leaders since "the concept of a single leader is not viable in the theocratic social structure of the Pueblo world."[1] Franklin Folsom offered a simpler refutation. He suggested that there was no "black man with yellow eyes," but rather that Chávez mistook reports of "a Pueblo ceremonial dancer who wore a black mask."[2]

Notes

1. Stefanie Beninato, "Popé, Pose-yemu, and Naranjo: A New Look at Leadership in the Pueblo Revolt of 1680," *New Mexico Historical Review* 65 (October 1990): 435. Andrew L. Knaut, *The Pueblo Revolt of 1680: Conquest and Resistance in Seventeenth-Century New Mexico* (Norman: University of Oklahoma Press, 1995), overlooks Beninato's article.

2. Franklin Folsom, *Red Power on the Rio Grande: The Native American Revolution of 1680,* intro. Alfonso Ortiz (1, 1973; reprint, Albuquerque: University of New Mexico Press, 1996), 132–33.

Questions for a Closer Reading

1. What characteristics did Pueblos have, in Chávez's judgment, that made them incapable of uniting against Spaniards?

2. Why does Chávez believe that mixed bloods like Domingo Naranjo could lead Pueblos more effectively than Pueblo leaders themselves?

3. Why does Chávez take his readers on an excursion into the subject of Pueblo religion?

4. Chávez's choice of words diminishes the Pueblos, their religion, and their leaders. What examples stand out in your mind?

5. What is the strongest evidence that Chávez offers to identify Domingo Naranjo of Santa Clara as the tall, black representative of Pohé-yemo?

6. What is the weakest evidence?

7. Why does Chávez relate the history of five generations of Naranjos, taking his readers far back in time before the Pueblo Revolt?

Pohé-yemo's Representative
and the Pueblo Revolt of 1680

The point of highest drama in New Mexico's long history is the Indian Pueblo Revolt of 1680, when the pueblos managed to unite briefly for one concerted effort which put an end to the Spanish colony and the Franciscan missions for a time. Twenty-one friars and several Spanish families were massacred in one day, August 10, and the Spaniards were soon forced to retreat to the distant and southernmost mission center of Guadalupe del Paso, now Ciudad Juárez in Mexico. The causes for the rebellion were several, but ancient pueblo belief was the one adduced by the main leaders as the rallying cry. It was the "ancient ones" of the pueblos versus the God and the saints of the Spaniards. For eighty years the Franciscans had clamored for the complete elimination of the estufas (now called kivas), which in their estimation were hotbeds of idolatry; also, that of the masked dances and related native practices which they considered not only idolatrous, but grossly immoral from the Christian point of view. These they lumped together under the term *cachinas*. Simply to provoke the missionaries, or else bribed by the Indian ritual leaders, certain Spaniards in the succession of governors and their henchmen refused to cooperate, so that the abolition of kivas and cachinas was occasional and sporadic; those eliminated were promptly restored in most pueblos.[1]

Such internal Church-State dissensions, to be sure, did nothing to improve the Indian ritual leaders' regard for the Spaniards. Moreover, and this is something never considered before by historians, some of the principal and most intelligent ones among the leaders were not pure-bred Pueblo Indians. Some were the offspring of an unscrupulous Spanish colonist and a pueblo woman; others were descended from Negroid-Amerindian servants, brought from New Spain by the first colonists, who married into the pueblos; and so during those first eighty years certain mestizos gravitated

Angélico Chávez, "Pohé-yemo's Representative and the Pueblo Revolt of 1680," *New Mexico Historical Review* 42 (1967): 85–126.

into pueblo life. A complicated inner resentment against the prevailing caste system had made them identify themselves further with the Pueblo Indian and his beliefs, while their native and acquired capabilities were superior to those of the inbred pueblos who knew little outside their individual restricted cosmos. Otherwise, the ordinary run of Pueblo Indians had been happy with the many material benefits brought them by the padres. Their limited grasp of Spanish Catholic doctrine and external worship dovetailed nicely with a native mythology which was their very life. They appreciated the protection which Spanish arms afforded against their perennial enemies, the Apache and other marauding tribes. In a way, for these common people, who in their simplicity had quietly combined interior ancestral belief with the external Catholic forms of worship, any demands made by the friars were less onerous than those made by their own ritual leaders, from whose complete influence they were being wooed. Native pueblo ritual and government required total surrender of the person.

It was the ritual leaders in each pueblo, the "representatives" of superior beings in a native mythology, which we will have to consider briefly, who resented European domination, no matter what the material benefits. The most resentful, and also potentially dangerous, were those hybrid leaders just mentioned. Nor can we eliminate a certain amount of laudable nativistic feeling on the part of the people in general, although it was far from the modern notion of "patriotism" anachronistically attributed to them by current American writers. Power and revenge, in the guise of native belief, were the prime motive. We might compare the situation with that of the fifteenth-century monarchy of Spain, with its closely interlaced feudal nobility and church hierarchy, which set up in the Inquisition under the banner of the Faith to consolidate and preserve its position against the divisive forces that it saw in the Moors, the Jews, and the Protestant Reformation. Except that these poor Indian leaders in the past had been altogether incapable of conjuring up any such Inquisition, or even a swift and definite revolution. The pueblo people in general, besides being satisfied with things as they were, were slow to respond to a war cry. Their agelong sedentary life of primitive agriculture and continuous ceremonial had made them a "peaceful people," seldom able to defend themselves against the warlike Apache hunters who from time immemorial had invaded the pueblos at harvest time. To stand up to Spanish firearms and European martial skills was suicidal, as some few found out on different occasions during that eighty-year period. Moreover, different pueblo groups were divided from each other by language and ancient animosities. And there was that internal struggle of long standing among the ritual leaders themselves in each pueblo, a fact noted by modern anthropologists as well as the pioneer missionaries.[2]

But the fact is that the many pueblos did manage to unite most effectively in that year of 1680, to the great surprise of the Spaniards, and to the wonder of serious historians ever since. In all subsequent histories the tactical genius has been thought to be El Popé of San Juan, from many scattered testimonies recorded in the Otermín journals of 1681. Yet, from the very start, Governor Otermín and his captains sensed that El Popé could not have done it all alone, and therefore tried to discover the chief culprit, or culprits, by interrogating their first prisoners. On August 9, 1680, two young men from Tesuque were caught bearing a message of rebellion and a hide thong with two knots signifying the number of days left. All that the frightened youths could reveal under pressure was a "common report among all the Indians that there had come to them from very far away toward the *north* a *letter* from an *Indian lieutenant* [*teniente*] *of Po he yemu* to the effect that all of them in general should rebel, and that any pueblo that would not agree to it they would destroy, killing all the people. It was reported that this *Indian lieutenant of Po he yemu was very tall, black, and had very large yellow eyes,* and that everyone feared him greatly."[3] The Spanish officials simply took this for a fable, concluding that the Indian leaders had deluded these youths and the people in general with this reference to one of their heathen "gods" or "spirits." It is evident that the young pair had divulged all they knew, and that Otermín and his men failed to detect a real human instigator behind their statement. For it certainly looked like the description of some grotesquely masked mythological creature which the Spaniards regarded as the "devil."

Again, a similar interrogation took place on August 20, after the Governor's forces broke a painful siege of Santa Fe by putting more than fifteen hundred warriors to rout, killing three hundred, and taking forty-seven prisoners. On being questioned, these unfortunate captives confessed that they "had a mandate of an *Indian* who lives a very long way from this kingdom, toward the *north*, from which region *Montezuma came*, and who is the *lieutenant of Po he yemu;* and that this *person* ordered all the Indians to take part in the treason and rebellion. . . . *For fear* of this they all joined together, killing the priests and the Spaniards. . . ."[4] Once again it is evident that this was all the poor prisoners knew, else at least one of the forty-seven would have revealed the identity of that "person." And again Otermín took this as an affront to his intelligence; in his anger he had them all shot for mocking him with a mere Indian fable. To him and his men the person of the *teniente* and *Pohé-yemo* himself were one and the same pagan demon.[5] But we shall soon see that he was a very human person — I shall translate *teniente* as "representative" from now on. It expresses more fully the double function of someone "taking the place of" and "assuming the person" of Pohé-yemo. The French-derived "lieutenant" has too many European military and political connotations.

What first led me to suspect a real human person in the Representative of Pohé-yemo, a man who was unusually tall and black in comparison with the average small and not too tawny Pueblo Indian, and one with big yellow eyes, which promptly suggests a mulatto, was the records of a controversy in Santa Fe in 1766. It involves five generations of the Naranjo family of the Santa Cruz–Santa Clara valley whose antecedents were Negroid and who, most significantly, were accused of having fomented Indian insurrections in the past.[6] Then, there is an amply documented legend, originating with the ordinary Spanish colonists of those Revolt times, which told of the Devil appearing as a black giant during the 1680 siege of Santa Fe.[7] All this provided me with enough incentive and material for a thorough investigation of the problem, concerned mainly with a big Negro or black-complexioned mulatto named Naranjo, who at some period before the Revolt of 1680 insinuated himself among the ritual leaders of the pueblos, several of them hybrid individuals like himself. Either to enjoy personal power, or to avenge himself on the Europeans who for so long, and sometimes most cruelly, had lorded it over the primitive colored races, or for both reasons, he most cleverly employed the myth of Pohé-yemo to unite the ever-dissident Pueblo Indians for a successful blow. It is not the first time that an African spoiled the best-laid plans of the Spaniard in American colonial times, but it was the most dramatic. More active and restless by nature than the more passive and stolid Indian, he was more apt to muddle up some serious Hispanic enterprise.[8]

In order to grasp the truth and flavor of the whole episode, we need to have some knowledge and sympathetic understanding of Pueblo Indian mythology and its workings on Indian behavior — in this case particularly concerning a mythical being called Pohé-yemo. This is something the captains and friars neglected to procure, to their sorrow. As they kept repeating in their official acts and letters, it was Satan himself and none other who had inspired the "apostasy and rebellion" against the twin Majesties of God and Catholic King.

1. *Pueblo Mythology and Pohé-yemo*

The daily life of the Pueblo Indians was closely and intricately bound with year-round rites and ceremonials intended to tap, as it were, the mysterious Power permeating their little world of earth and sky.[9] The Power was impersonal, nothing more than the invisible energy that made nature tick. Each pueblo's cosmos was limited to the visible horizon around it. Upon the earth the Power made trees and plants grow, and the wild animals to reproduce themselves; and from the sky above the Power supplied sunlight and rain, all to insure a food supply for the people in their planting and hunting. Also, through herbs and animals the Power furnished means for curing the people when sick. Naturally, the Power also made human babies grow from their parents to insure the continuity of the community. And, as with other primitives, there was a division of the Power's activities into male and female: sky phenomena were masculine as compared with the passive feminine reproduction in the earth. Hence fertility rites acquired certain open sexual manifestations, pointed out by ethnologists, and by some of the old padres who naturally labeled them obscene.

Because the Power was so erratic in its activities, mainly as regards rainfall and fertility in an arid land, what was needed to insure good crops, good hunting, a healthy people and healthy newborn, was the right effective knowledge, or "know-how," that could make the Power work in their behalf. All that one needed was "to know." This "know-how" rested in their ritual leaders, the Representative Chieftains and Medicinemen, to whom it had been passed down through countless generations from the "ancient ones" since the Pueblo People came out of the earth. The ritual leaders, according to each one's office, prepared themselves by purificatory bathing, fasting, and considerable vomiting, in order to better "represent" the "ancient ones" in putting the "know-how" to work. The better the preparation, the closer a leader came to "becoming" an "ancient one" for that particular function. And the greater the results.

Now, the pueblos had no Creation Myth. Their ancestors came out of a Hole, or vertical Cave, in the already existing earth. It lay somewhere beyond the northern horizon of each pueblo's little world. These first people were as ignorant and helpless as babies emerging from the womb. But just as helpless infants have parents and adult clan relatives to assist them through childhood, so the first people encountered other people, and also animals, who were ready to help and teach them. These were the "ancient ones." These primordial counterparts of the ordinary human and animal world were real corporeal beings. They differed from ordinary folk and animals in this one important respect — they had a perfect "know-how" for using the Power. Through this perfect knowledge they made themselves immortal, and they could perform all sorts of marvelous feats, like making themselves invisible and changing from one place to another in the twinkling of an eye. This instant travel was sometimes done with the aid of primordial birds and animals having the same "know-how." Each one of them specialized in the phenomena of one distinct phase of nature.

These benign "ancient ones" stayed with those first people and taught them how to plant and hunt and fend for themselves. Those who were animals taught them the art of curing with herbs and chants. But there were skeptics even in those days, folks who said the "ancient ones" were nothing but ordinary people disguised in masks and paint and feathers. This unbelief hurt those benefactors, so they decided to go away from the ordinary people forever. But, before departing, they taught the true believers how to use their masks and perform dances with them, and how to employ other paraphernalia such as feather bunches, feathered sticks, and tiny stone fetishes, and how to sing the right songs, to make sure that the people would always have a means of tapping the Power for corn and meat and health, even if in a much more limited degree.

Chief among these kindly beings were the Earth-Mother (*Yaya*) who dwelt by the Hole of Emergence (*Shipapu*), and the Twin-Warriors and Hunters (*Másewi* and *Oyóyewi*), who stayed with her but frequently roamed all over. Most popular were the *Shiwanna* or Rain-Makers who dwelt beyond the western horizon, or some other direction, depending on a particular pueblo's location with regard to prevailing rain clouds. Among these many single individuals controlling some phase of nature was *Pohé-yemo*, who made the sun shine upon the people when they first came out upon the dark and dreary earth's surface. He and the other beings varied in name, concept, and particular functions among the different pueblos, and even in those of the same linguistic group.[10]

Pohé-yemo is called *Pose-yemo* among the Tewa (Santa Clara where Naranjo lived). It means "he who strews morning dew." Another name is *Pose-ueve* (dew from sky), but he is also referred to as *Pose-yemo T'ansendo* (our sun father *Pose-yemo*). The Keres of Santo Domingo know these Tewa terms but also have their own: *Payatyamo* (youth) who is the being in charge of the sun. In Cochiti *Payatyama* (sun-father) is used in contradistinction to *Sanatyaya* (moon-mother), but in action he is identified with *Oshatsh*, the sun. Both in Santo Domingo and San Felipe, *Payatyamo* appears among the fetishes used in preparing for the cachina dances. There are two masks among those of the minor side-dancers which are called *Payatyamo*, resembling the mask of the sun, *Oshatsh*. Dances originally performed for *Payatyamo* now are directed to the Rain-Makers, both at Santo Domingo and Cochiti. From this and other instances, it is clear that the person of the sun-youth was considerably less "performed" than those of the bringers of rain, and this is very natural. In the arid Southwest the sun shines perennially, and therefore needs much less invoking than those beings who control the much needed rain clouds, or those who cause the corn to grow and the wild game to multiply abundantly. Santo Domingo also uses the term *Poshaiyanyi* (our father from east coming with sun), but this is plainly a derivation from the Zuñi *Poshaiyankia*. He is the being who taught the Zuñi, the Taos, and other peoples, the arts of planting and ceremonial curing. Among the Jemez, *Pestya-sode* figures in a legend similar to one among the Zuñi, the prefix *pe* meaning "sun" in their language. But they also use *Peyat-yambo* (their version of Keres "youth") for the ritual leader of the Pecos sun clan. The mask of *Pehehmiyoe* (sun on head) has features of the Keres sun-mask, *Oshatsh*.

In short, the original concept of this youth and father having the "know-how" of the sun has not only gotten mixed up in linguistic form but also in the "know-how" pertaining to other mythical persons. He also figures in later tales of the Zuñi, Jemez, Tewa, and Keres, as relayed by investigators like Bandelier and Cushing, but these are more properly current folktales than old ancestral mythology. What we have been arriving at is the fact that, in that fateful year of 1680, all the pueblos knew of Pohé-yemo under one linguistic form or another, when word came from a kiva in Taos that a Chieftain or Medicineman therein had a most extraordinary "know-how" of Pohé-yemo and was *representing* him. In performing the preparatory rites he must have fasted and vomited so effectively that he now represented Pohé-yemo to perfection — he *was* Pohé-yemo at this time. El Popé and the few select leaders let the people know that he was a black giant with big yellow eyes for greater effect. This created more than the usual fear and awe. His human identity was of no consequence, for at the time he fully represented Pohé-yemo.

Why Naranjo chose to represent Pohé-yemo instead of the mighty Twin-Warriors, *Másewi* and *Oyóyewi*, we do not know. But we can guess. It could be the connotation of "sun" with "fire." For Naranjo himself knew of the Aztec god of Fire and War, as we shall see later on. Reared among the Spaniards and cognizant of the real Indian idolatry of New Spain, he imbued his self-assumed mysterious personality with a cruel inner strength unknown to the placid and less sophisticated pueblos. He could communicate with some of the principal leaders in their own tongue, but also in Spanish with those outstanding ones who were mestizos and *coyotes;* and to some of these he could send written letters. His grasp of Spanish psychology showed him how to catch the enemy off guard, and how to hide his identity from them in case the plot should fail, as it almost did. Because the captains as well as the padres looked upon the "ancient ones" of the pueblos as the evil spirits given in the Bible, Pohé-yemo would be regarded as the Devil himself. And so he was.

The blow fell on August 10, 1680, and the success was almost perfect, marred only by the bloody resistance of the Spaniards in Santa Fe. Governor Otermín and his people held on to the villa for a spell, but considered it wise to abandon it and the whole kingdom for the time being. In his questioning of Indian captives, for future reprisals, Otermín got nothing from them, even when they unwittingly described Naranjo physically. For he had made his personal identity known only to a few main leaders, perhaps instructing them not to reveal it to the pueblo people in general. But as soon as the Spaniards left, the pueblos fell away from each other, forgetting all about Pohé-yemo's Representative. For the deed was done. And no ritual leader, after all, could "represent" an "ancient one" indefinitely. At the same time the other ritual leaders of separate pueblos assumed their own little stances of importance, especially El Popé, who went about boasting that he alone had at last defeated the invincible Spaniard and restored the influence of the "ancient ones." Many among the common people did not like this new surge of tyranny, which now had more of a sharp European flavor than the halcyon former rule of the "ancient ones." If Naranjo himself had harbored any ambition of making himself the supreme lord of all the pueblos, it was a rude awakening.

Otermín's return with his forces in the following year was largely one of reconnaissance. Individual Indians of every type were captured from among the southern Rio Grande pueblos, then questioned minutely as to the leaders and causes of the Revolt. The governor's findings were mostly a confirmation of what he had heard the previous year, and these were written down by his clerks in Spanish Christian terms and concepts. One old Indian of Alameda said that Indian resentment had built up from the very beginning of the colony and missions, because the friars and Spaniards took away their *idols* and forbade *sorceries and idolatries.*[11] Another accused El Popé of San Juan, whom all feared because he *talked with the devil;* he killed his own son-in-law, who was the (Spanish-imposed) governor of San Juan, because he was too friendly with the Spaniards and might reveal the plot to them. He went about with El Saca of Taos boasting that he alone had carried out the uprising, and proclaiming that the *devil was very strong and much better than God.*[12] Another told a captain that El Popé had made all the Indians crazy and was like the whirlwind. He had given them to understand that the *father of all the Indians, their great chieftain, who had been such since the Deluge,* had ordered El Popé to make all the pueblos rebel, or else be laid waste.[13] Still others declared that the rebellion had been motivated by the Taos and El Popé, whom all regarded as a *great sorcerer,* and who presented himself as a great chieftain. He went about destroying Christian vestiges and enforcing the ancient customs.[14] Friars and captains wrote that it all was the result of *diabolical* cunning and conspiracy, discord which *the devil had sown,* apostasy caused by *blind fiends of the devil.* After eighty years of baptism, the *most intelligent and favored* among them, with complete secrecy, acted as the moving spirits and guides.[15] They pointed out some of these intelligent leaders: besides El Popé there were Alonso Catiti, *coyote* of Santo Domingo, Luis and Lorenzo Tupatu of Picuris, Nicolás Jonva, and Francisco El Ollita, *coyote* of San Ildefonso. But nobody mentioned a certain Naranjo, the *negro* or *mulato* of Santa Clara operating from a kiva in Taos. His identity had been kept too well hidden except for that dangerously close description of the previous year: a black giant with big yellow eyes. However, certain Naranjo individuals did enter the picture at this time, and these will now be treated more at length as we work out the Naranjo family relationship.

2. *The Naranjo Family*

In the year 1766, the colonial militia officials of Santa Fe and Santa Cruz were up in arms because a certain José Antonio Naranjo claimed to be, by a title conferred by the Viceroy, the overall field commander of colonial troops in New Mexico. At the moment Governor Vélez Cachupín had acknowledged the claim on the basis of documents which Naranjo had presented purporting to prove that not only he, but his father, grandfather, and great-grandfather before him, had received the title from successive Viceroys in Mexico City. Furthermore, his great-grandfather had been a first Conquistador of the kingdom. The Spanish officers countered by saying that the military title in question was that of *Capitán Mayor de Guerra* for auxiliary Indian troops only, not for Spaniards, that Naranjo's remote ancestors were not Spanish Conquistadores but a Negro slave and an Indian female servant, and that his subsequent black ancestors in the line had been the instigators of Indian uprisings in the past. Governor Cachupín then reviewed the case by interrogating witnesses, and by examining the archives in Santa Fe and the papers in Naranjo's possession. From all this we have a good picture of five generations of the Naranjo family, which are first stated briefly for greater clarity, then considered singly in full detail.

(1) The original ancestor, when the New Mexico colony was founded (1598–1600), was a very black Negro slave or servant, married to a female Indian servant. (2) They had a son, Domingo Naranjo, who was born after the Conquest and was involved in Indian uprisings. (3) Domingo's son, José (López) Naranjo, attached himself to the Reconquistador Vargas (1692) and became a Major War-Captain of Indian auxiliary troops. (4) His son, José Antonio Naranjo, also held the same position and title. (5) His son, José Antonio Naranjo (II), the man making these outlandish claims in 1766, enjoyed the same title, but for Indian troops only, and was a consummate rascal and livestock rustler besides.[16] Now we can proceed to identify each generation according to the minute evidence offered in this case, as also from many other sources, in our endeavor to pin down the Naranjo who was the Representative of Pohé-yemo in 1680.

First Generation: The anonymous Negro and his anonymous Indian wife. All that we know from this investigation of 1766 is that he was a very black-complexioned Negro (*negro atezado*), a slave or servant who married an Indian *criada* of Juana de los Reyes, the wife of an original New Mexico settler of the Martines family.[17] There is only one male Negroid servant mentioned in the Oñate papers, 1597–1600. It is a most interesting single document concerning a recently freed mulatto who did come in the expedition of 1600 as a squire to a minor officer, Juan Bautista Ruano. He is described as a *mulato* by the name of *Mateo,* twenty years of age, "a tall man branded on the face as a slave and with other letters not well outlined," who presented an affidavit from his former master. It gave him his freedom on the sole condition that he serve his Majesty by joining the expedition going to New Mexico in 1600. His generous master had been Mateo Montero, resident of Puebla de los Angeles, who had purchased him from Alonso de la Torre, resident of the mines of Pachuca. The instrument was officially executed in the city of Los Angeles on January 26, 1600.[18] The soldier, Juan Bautista Ruano, did not stay in New Mexico, but Mateo was obliged to remain under the stipulations of his freedom papers. Hence he must have entered the service of another soldier who settled in the new land.

There was a soldier in this same expedition by the name of *Alonso Martines,* or *Martín,* a native of Higuera de Vargas in Estremadura, the son of Benito Díaz, with complete armor for himself and steed. In all he had 10 horses, 24 cows, and many household chattels,[19] more than many an unattached officer or soldier had. He is also referred to as Alonso Martín *Naranjo.*[20] No wife is mentioned, as with other settlers, but his many household possessions suggest that he did have one, by the name of Juana de los Reyes, who could have been overlooked when the muster rolls were drawn up. Or else he acquired one not long thereafter, perhaps a Spanish colonist's daughter. Or, from the name "Juana de los Reyes," we might suppose that he married along the way a Mexican Indian servant, of which there was a supply. (Juan Bautista Ruano had also brought along two Indian women, one of them called "Juana," who had left her man in New Spain.) At any rate, it does seem that Mateo became Naranjo's *peón,* for when Governor Oñate's activities were being investigated down in Mexico City in 1601, his chief auditor testified that Oñate's livestock at a pueblo called Santa Clara was in the care of "a certain Naranjo."[21] Since the auditor could not recall the man's first name, and since the independent character of those colonial soldiers would not let them stoop to be Oñate's herders (nor could they be spared for such menial tasks), it seems as though our mulatto Mateo is being referred to here. All this is mere reasoned supposition, yet it fits well with subsequent facts, such as the eventual settlement of the black Naranjos in the environs of Santa Clara.

A similar hypothesis may be advanced regarding Mateo's wife. In addition to Ruano's two Mexican Indian women, there is another one by the name of María, who was brought by the soldier Juan López. She is mentioned again in a list of female servants as presented by their respective masters, and most of these women seem to be of low caste. But there are three

Tlascaltec sisters who stand out above the rest for being the daughters of a Don Joseph of Tepeaca. They were brought along by Juan López. One was *María,* unmarried, with a little daughter Mariana; the other was Catalina, unmarried, with a child called María; the third was Agustina, married to the Indian Francisco, also a servant of Juan López.[22] Whether or not this Juan López stayed in New Mexico, we do not know. But in either case María, if not Catalina, could have joined the household of Alonso Martín Naranjo and thus come to marry Mateo, who was in the same employ. What is more, Mateo had lived in Puebla, and she was from Tepeaca nearby. They could have become well acquainted during the long trek north, if they had not known each other before. This supposition rests not only on the fact that a notorious grandson sometimes used the double surname of *López* Naranjo, but on the superior vitality, sagacity, and intelligence displayed by some of their descendants down several generations. The girls were the daughters of *Don* Joseph, which means that he was a major Tlascaltec chieftain or governor who had been found worthy to use such a title by the officialdom of New Spain; perhaps the girls had been left orphans and destitute, and so were persuaded by Juan López to find a new life in New Mexico. The marriage of one to tall Mateo, whose personality and intelligence must have prompted his kind master to grant him his freedom, insured a very superior progeny. It also serves to explain why the Representative of Pohé-yemo was so conversant with Mexican Indian lore in all his crafty dealings.

Second Generation: Domingo Naranjo, son of the *negro atezado* [Mateo Naranjo] and of [María or Catalina López], Indian house-girl (*criada*) of Juana de los Reyes of the Martines [Naranjo] family. In 1766 Domingo's great-grandson claimed that he had been one of the Spanish Conquistadores of the kingdom, that he had received the title of *Capitán Mayor de la Guerra,* and that his son Joseph (López) Naranjo had succeeded him in office.[23] Not so, said the Spanish officers of the colonial militia. Domingo, the *tronco* of these rebellious Naranjos of Santa Clara, could not have been a Conquistador since he was the son of *un negro atezado y una india criada* of a Martines housewife. These Naranjo ancestors came as slaves or servants of the first conquerors and settlers. The greatest honor that Domingo Naranjo ever enjoyed — and this is most unlikely — was to be the Chief War-Captain of Indians, not of Spaniards. There were no Naranjos with any titles to be found in Otermín's lists of colonists at the time of the Revolt of 1680, declared Governor Cachupín after consulting the archives.[24] This is all we know about Domingo Naranjo as such. He appears by name in no other documents that might identify him as the tall black Representative of Pohé-yemo with the big yellow eyes. But the times and topography point directly to him as the black Tewa of Santa Clara who, sometime before 1680, hid himself in a kiva of Taos to plot and carry out the terrible rebellion of that year.

We do, however, meet with a contemporary bearing the name *Pedro* Naranjo. When Governor Otermín reached the pueblo of Isleta in his reconnaissance expedition of 1681, his men arrested a very old Indian who gave this as his name; he was found to be a great sorcerer who had come down from the upper pueblos to teach his superstitions. In order to gather more evidence against him, Otermín dispatched troops to reconnoiter the upper pueblos.[25] Old Naranjo claimed that he was a Keres of San Felipe, yet he spoke not only Keres and Tewa (of Santa Clara!), but made himself very well understood in Castilian. He understood the nature of an oath and formally took it when questioned on December 18; and his knowledge of Spanish-Indian relations in the past decades is most revealing.[26] He said that since the days of Governor Ugarte y de la Concha (1650), the pueblos had planned rebellions on various occasions through the conspiracy of Indian sorcerers.[27] The message was accepted in some pueblos, but not in others, so they failed. Seven or eight Indians were hanged as a result, and the unrest subsided. Sometime thereafter, "they" sent from Taos to all the pueblos two deerskins with pictures painted on them calling for a new rebellion.[28] The deerskins went as far as the Hopi pueblos, which refused to accept them, and the rebellion failed once more. But the idea "was kept in their hearts." Finally it materialized under El Popé, who was said to have *communication with the devil.* "It happened that in an estufa of the pueblo of Los Taos there appeared to the said Popé *three figures of Indians* who never came out of the estufa. They gave the said Popé to understand that they were going underground to the *lake of Copala.* He saw these figures *emit fire* from the extremities of their body, and that one of them was called *Caudi,* another *Tilini,* and the other *Tleume,* and those three beings spoke to the said Popé, who was in hiding from the secretary Francisco Xavier,[29] who wished to punish him as a sorcerer. They told him to make a *cord of maguey fiber* and tie some knots in it,[30] which would signify the number of days that they must wait for the rebellion." After relating how the knotted cord had gone from pueblo to pueblo, Naranjo told how a proclamation went forth for all the pueblos to obey the command of their *"father whom they did not know,*[31] which would be given either through *El Caydi* or El Popé." Alonso Catiti brought the message from Santo Domingo to San Felipe, with orders that those who disobeyed would be *beheaded.*[32] The reason for rebelling, Naranjo went on, was "because they had always desired to live as they had when they came out of the lake of *Copala.*" After the Spaniards departed, El Popé went about telling the pueblos to break all images, bells, and crosses, to wash off the water and holy oils of baptism by bathing in the river with yucca-root soap, and to *put away their wives and take on new ones.*[33] This mandate came from *El*

Caydi and the other two spirits in the Taos kiva who emitted fire, and the Indians "thereby returned to the state of antiquity, as when they came from the *lake of Copala*." Those Christian Indians who refused were killed by orders of El Popé. To further terrorize the others, El Popé and the *three demons* announced that any Indian harboring any affection for the priests and the Spaniards would be promptly executed. *The demons in the Taos kiva* also said that if the Spaniards ever returned, all the pueblos would fight to the death. The demons would issue a warning as soon as the Spaniards started out for the north. Pedro Naranjo finished his testimony by saying that he had come to the southern pueblos out of fear (!) to teach them idolatrous dances, "in which he greatly fears in his heart that he may have offended God, and that now *having been absolved and returned to the fold* of the church, he has spoken the truth." He gave his age as eighty, and *signed his name* to the declaration.[34]

Pedro Naranjo's testimony is purposely given here in detail, and with several words and phrases in italics, to show that here was no mere Pueblo Indian speaking in pueblo terms and concepts, but a man well versed by birth and upbringing in matters wholly foreign to pueblo mentality. He seems to have been lying when he said he was a native Keres of San Felipe, and one cannot help but suspect that he also altered his name a bit, that he actually was Domingo Naranjo of Santa Clara.—And yet we would think that Domingo's unusual size, his Negroid color and features, and his yellow eyes, should have made the Spaniards suspect that he was not a San Felipe Keres. Hence it could well be that Pedro Naranjo was Domingo's brother, smaller in stature and more Indian in appearance, and was his agent in the southern pueblos.—How he slyly tried to steer the Spaniards away from the Representative of Pohé-yemo (himself or his brother) is evident from the three spirits he now invented. To say, as the prisoners questioned at the time of the Revolt did, that the coordinator of it was a black giant with big yellow eyes would be coming too close for comfort. Therefore, it was *El Caudi, Tilini,* and *Tleume* emitting fire from their extremities—names that have the sound and look of Nahuatl rather than of any of the pueblo tongues. They also suggest, more specifically, the Aztec god of Fire and War.[35] Then there is Pedro Naranjo's reference more than once to the lake of Copala, which he confuses with the Pueblo Indians' *Shipapu* or Hole-in-the-earth whence their ancestors emerged, thus also making it an underground lake. (Allied to this concept is that reference the year before about a far place to the north whence *Montezuma* came.) In all the Revolt annals Pedro Naranjo is the only one who mentions the three spirits and the lake of Copala. Nor does the word "Copala" figure in connection with New Mexico pueblo myth. Here we have a Hispanic-Indian concoction from New Spain being grafted onto pueblo mythology. It had to come from the Mexican Indians in general; specifically, from Naranjo's own parents and the New World Spanish milieu in which he and his parents grew up.[36]

Finally, we have Pedro Naranjo's age of eighty, his ability to sign his name, his thorough grasp of the nature of an oath, his ability to make a well ordered (if fraudulent) sacramental confession to Father Ayeta. His age places his birth at San Gabriel (or Santa Clara) in the beginning of the century, perhaps the first-born of the mulatto-Tlascaltec couple. His literacy and easy familiarity with Spanish civil and religious practices set him apart from the illiterate pueblo natives who at best had but a vague comprehension of Spanish Catholic practices. For the only "Pueblo Indians" conversant with writing and such practices at this period were some of the Mexican Indians among them, like the faithful Bartolomé de Ojeda at Zia, for example, whose full Spanish names and surnames identify them as non-pueblo Indian in origin, and some of the resentful rebel *mestizos, coyotes,* and *lobos* who carried out the Revolt for Naranjo in their respective pueblos. But still the actual Representative of Pohé-yemo, the Naranjo individual from Santa Clara who went to Taos and from there engineered the rebellion under this clever mystic guise, remains to be fully identified. Apparently his name was Domingo Naranjo. But were Domingo and Pedro the same man?

Third Generation: Joseph (López) Naranjo, son of Domingo Naranjo. As young men, he and his brother Lucas (whom he killed years later) might have had some active part in the Revolt of 1680. Their own children could not, of course. But these succeeding generations have to be considered here for the light which their testimonies and lives throw on Pohé-yemo's Representative. Joseph Naranjo, his grandson claimed in 1766, had succeeded his father Domingo as Major War-Captain (not true). He received his title from the Viceroy Duque de Linares and also performed outstanding deeds for the kingdom of New Mexico (true).[37] But, protested the Spanish officers, he was war-captain for Indian auxiliaries only, because he was not even Spanish. One witness who remembered knowing Joseph said that his complexion was decidedly black and that he was nicknamed *"el Mulato."* Another also remembered his color as black, and that some called him *"el Negro,"* others *"el Mulato."*[38] In bewilderment Governor Cachupín consulted the archives, then declared that the only Naranjos he could find therein were an Indian Naranjo (Pedro) whom Otermín found at Isleta, and among the Keres two mulatto brothers also called Naranjo.[39] If Cachupín had perused these Otermín *autos* of 1681 more studiously, he might have detected among them a certain bright young Spanish-speaking Indian by the name of *Josephe.*

After sly old Pedro Naranjo was arrested at Isleta on December 8, 1681, Otermín sent some men up to San Felipe in order to find more evidence against him. On December 18 Juan Domínguez brought in five prisoners to the Governor, who was then encamped in the Alameda-Sandía area. These captives were Juan of Tesuque; *Josephe,* a Spanish-speaking youth who did not reveal his tribe; *Lucas,* who claimed to be a Piro from Socorro; and *two mulatto lads* called Juan Lorenzo and Francisco Lorenzo, who lived with their mother near San Felipe, and whose elder brother, Bartolomé Naranjo, had been killed by the San Felipe Indians during the Revolt.[40] It is very significant that the depositions of Josephe, Lucas, and Pedro Naranjo were taken in this order on December 19, and then those of the two Lorenzo brothers on the following day, all in succession.

Josephe, without offering a surname or his pueblo, or even hinting that he knew his captured companions, stated in good Spanish that he had been an employed servant of the Sargento Mayor Sebastián de Herrera when the Revolt broke out.[41] He said that he had joined the Spanish refugees going down to Guadalupe del Paso, but many months later he ran away from La Toma (Real de San Lorenzo) with another young Indian called Domingo. When they got back to the northern pueblos, the rebels executed Domingo because they had seen him fighting on the Spanish side during the siege of Santa Fe. Now, said Josephe, he had voluntarily rejoined the Spaniards to warn them of Indian treachery after they had made peace offers. As the instigators of the Revolt he named El Popé and other pueblo leaders of San Juan, Taos, and San Ildefonso. He did not mention any leader from Santa Clara. To the interrogator he seemed to be about twenty years old, but could well have been younger. He did not know how to sign his name.

His declaration was followed by that of Lucas, who looked to be more than twenty years old, and who claimed to be a Piro of Socorro captured by the rebels. He knew only the Piro language, he said. He swore through an interpreter that he did not know who had plotted the Revolt; the Tiwa of Isleta had picked up him and his companions by orders of a chief — "he does not know who he is." He had but recently joined the Keres, yet he understood the details of their current plotting without knowing their language. He had surrendered voluntarily because a brother of his was with the Otermín forces and had sent word ahead for Lucas to join him. This shifty character is pointed out here for being circumstantially allied with Josephe and with Pedro Naranjo, although acting as a stranger to both[42] — and because Joseph Naranjo had a brother Lucas whom he slew during a subsequent rebellion.

Old Pedro Naranjo was interviewed next, and it was a long process as we have seen, which left the two mulatto brothers for questioning the following day.[43] These are also important to know, since they have some bearing on the Naranjo relationship, a branch of which was not on the side of the rebels. Their names were Juan Lorenzo and Francisco Lorenzo, and they spoke good Spanish. When the Revolt broke out they were living with their mother at a little rancho near San Felipe, not in the pueblo itself. They had gone to the pueblo on that fateful day of August 10, 1680, to hear Mass in honor of St. Lawrence, when their elder brother Bartolomé Naranjo arrived from somewhere and began upbraiding the San Felipes for rebelling. For this they pounced upon him and killed him with their war clubs. This faithful Christian Naranjo was in all probability the young man working in Santa Fe whom Governor Otermín had sent down to San Felipe to inquire about the state of affairs in the southern pueblos.[44] The two boys did not implicate any Naranjos, only El Popé, most likely because they did not know anything else. If they did know old Pedro Naranjo, they could have kept silent out of fear. In this connection there was another Naranjo by the name of Pascual, who had lived with his family in the Analco ward of Santa Fe. He could well have been an uncle of the slain Bartolomé, by being the brother of the woman living just outside of San Felipe with her two Lorenzo youngsters by a different man or husband. For all were referred to as mulattoes, and a mulatto of the previous generation had resided at a rancho called Tunque near San Felipe.[45] The inference is that only the immediate family of Domingo and/or Pedro Naranjo was connected with the Revolt, while the other kin remained faithful to the Spaniards and the Faith. Because of their length these complicated matters, like other arguments previously offered, are relegated to the notes.

To get back to Joseph Naranjo, or Josephe, we meet him a full decade later under similar circumstances. On January 8, 1682, Josephe and Juan of Tesuque had escaped from Otermín's party on its way back to Guadalupe del Paso, and had fled once more to the northern pueblos.[46] Possibly fearing retaliation from the Keres and the Tewas, Josephe went to live in Taos — where his father Domingo Naranjo had directed the Revolt and perhaps was still there. For here the army of Governor Vargas encountered him on October 7, 1692. The pueblo of Taos was found abandoned, but after a while two Indians came down from the mountains to parley with Vargas.[47] One was the governor of the Taos, Francisco Pacheco.[48] The other was a young Indian *ladino* (meaning very glib in Spanish) who called himself *Josephillo* (little Joe) and was referred to by the Taos as "el Español" because of his proficiency in the language. (And very possibly because the Taos Tiwas knew that he was not a Pueblo Indian, but descended from alien people who had come with the Spanish colonists.) For some reason, Governor Vargas took an immediate liking to him, showing him many kindnesses at their first meeting, and from this moment on Josephe or Josephillo cast his lot for good with the Spaniards.[49] After a decade of vacillating between loyalty to the native pueblos and to the Spaniards, he saw a brighter personal future with the latter.

His "peaceful Entrada" of 1692 accomplished, Vargas returned to Guadalupe del Paso with his army, and we presume that Josephillo went along,[50] to return with the army and the colonists in the second Vargas Entrada of 1693. In this final entry into New Mexico, Vargas soon discovered that his easy "pacification" of the previous year was only a delusion. Serious signs of resistance appeared everywhere, but especially in the northern pueblos. He learned that the leaders were the brothers Luis and Lorenzo Tupatú of Picuris, Antonio Bolsas of the Tano Indians occupying Santa Fe, and "el mulato Naranjo del pueblo de Santa Clara."[51] This turned out to be Lucas Naranjo, brother of Joseph, who was to engineer the new Revolt of the Tewas in 1696 and the martyrdom of five more Franciscans, and then meet his end at the hands of his brother. Although Joseph is not mentioned in these 1693 annals, he must have witnessed the battle for Santa Fe and the defeat of the Tano and their Tewa and Tiwa allies. Most likely he accompanied Vargas and his forces in the various sorties that followed up until the next major outbreak in 1696. In this year he was living in the brand-new villa of Santa Cruz. On June 5 the five missionaries were slain, as also were several of the colonists; the Indians of most of the Rio Grande pueblos then fled up to their nearby mountain fastnesses. On June 13, when Joseph Naranjo and other men of Santa Cruz were gathering wood near the swollen Rio Grande, an Indian came down and confided to him that the combined Hopi, Zuñi, and Acoma were returning to help the local pueblos to destroy the Spaniards as soon as the river current subsided. Naranjo then notified the Alcalde of Santa Cruz, Roque de Madrid, to whom he had attached himself, and a general alarm was given.[52] Joseph must have known that his brother Lucas at Santa Clara was at the head of the new rebellion, or else he learned of it for sure from various testimonies taken from prisoners when the alarm was spread.[53]

This presented him with a wonderful opportunity to further ingratiate himself with Governor Vargas and with his mentor, Roque de Madrid. Somehow he managed to find his brother and killed him; then he cut off his head and presented it to Vargas. This act likewise put an end to this rebellion. As Joseph's grandson boasted in 1766, it was a heroic act which was officially certified by the Cabildo of Santa Fe, when "he killed his brother Lucas in the sorry uprising of the Tewa whom he headed, cutting the head off him and presenting it to the Governor; with the deed the rebels subsided." But a Spanish officer of 1766 countered by saying that the action was not so heroic, since Joseph Naranjo thus erased the infamy of his past life, and likewise got himself pardoned for having lived as an apostate among the gentile Apache of El Cuartelejo for many years, and cohabiting with an Apache squaw; there is where he learned other Indian languages.[54] But from then on Joseph Naranjo's rise among the Spaniards was swift and effective.

By 1700 he was Alcalde Mayor of Zuñi, when he went with the padre to the Hopi pueblos to confer with the mestizo Espeleta, leader of the Hopi.[55] The following year he formulated a petition which is extraordinarily revealing. It betrays long-harbored ambitions, born perhaps on the day when Vargas took him under his wing. Just as he had the bloody execution of his brother certified by the Santa Fe Cabildo, now in 1701 he approached the Franciscan Custos, Fray Antonio Guerra, asking him to write up his past accomplishments. His purpose, as it turned out, was to get the title of Chief War-Captain over all Indian troops from the Viceroy himself. He began by stating that he was "a native of the kingdom," and had already served his Majesty as Alcalde Mayor and War-Captain of Acoma and Zuñi. When he first got these titles from the Governor, the Acoma and Laguna were entrenched on the great rock of Acoma, and the Zuñi on their own fortress mountain, and he all alone persuaded the Laguna and the Zuñi to come down and return to their pueblos. No Spaniard helped him — only his own Christian zeal! (Joseph, unlike his grandson, was not trying to pass himself off as a Spaniard.) Then the Governor in Santa Fe ordered him to enter the ferocious Hopi nation, which he did with the Custos, Father Zavaleta, and with Father Garaycoechea of Zuñi and Father Miranda of Acoma. The party was sorely threatened by the Hopi, but he effectively defended the fathers at the risk of his life. When the Santa Clara Tewa on the rock of Walpi showed signs of surrender, he went up there against the prudent advice of the padres, and brought these people back to Santa Fe. Again, he returned to Walpi with Father Garaycoechea to bring back the Tano Indians living there. The good father tried to dissuade him from risking his life but he, after making his confession, bravely went up and argued with the Tano all night in their kiva; he could not persuade them to return to their pueblos, yet he got them to make peace with the Spaniards. Of the families he himself brought back from the Hopi pueblos, eight were Santa Claras now living in San Juan, six were San Ildefonsos, nine were Cochiti, four were Santo Domingos, six were Galisteos, and also the entire Jemez population now living in the pueblo. All this was done at his own expense without royal aid, as the friars who went with him could testify. This declaration he asked Father Guerra to certify formally, and with the signature and rubric of Joseph Naranjo.[56]

This is followed by an order from the Custos for Fathers Miranda and Garaycoechea to confirm it, and they do in glowing terms, affixing their signatures. Next is a previous certification by Governor Pedro Rodríguez Cubero, who states that Joseph Naranjo, vecino of this kingdom, requested of him the titles of Alcalde Mayor and Capitán de Guerra of Taos when for a year no one had dared go near the pueblo; upon receiving the titles, Naranjo went there and the natives were instructed in the Faith; he not only persuaded the Taos to receive Father Álvarez as their missionary, but got them to help him build the church before the padre got there. Therefore he is found worthy of any honor and grants which the King might choose to bestow on him. This statement is purportedly signed and sealed with his arms in Santa Fe, December 18, 1798 [1698].[57]

This declaration and the several certifications were obviously intended to obtain a more ambitious title as Chief War-Captain of all pueblo auxiliary troops, and he evidently did get it from the Duke of Linares. For this is not contradicted in a statement made by Naranjo before interim Governor Valverde y Cosío, August 13, 1719, that he was *Cabeza Mayor de la Guerra con título y nombramiento que hizo el Exmo. Virrey que fue, duque de Linares;* nor in another, June 2, 1720, *Capitán . . . que lo es Mayor de la Guerra de los naturales de este Reino, con título del Superior Gobierno.*[58] This last quotation also shows that the title of War-Captain was meant to be for Indian warriors only, and that Joseph did not claim command over Spanish soldiers and militiamen. Nevertheless, it was indeed a high and noteworthy position, for no individual "Indian" had ever exercised a general command over all pueblo auxiliary troops.

Nor do subsequent documents imply that his petition of 1701 contained empty boasts. In February 1702 he was still Alcalde Mayor of Zuñi, and very hopeful of reducing the Hopi to Christianity.[59] In March of the same year he and his pueblo troops were on a campaign under Captain Juan de Ulibarrí, when he declared having heard from the Acoma and Laguna Indians that the Zuñi and Hopi were passing around a "knotted thong" (*correa*). At this time he gave his age as thirty-five (probably off by several years), and he did not sign his name for not knowing how.[60] On March 4, 1703, the Zuñi killed three Spanish vecinos in their pueblo. At the time the soldiers and Naranjo were away, and on March 7 Father Garaycoechea wrote to Governor Cubero that the rebels were lying in wait night and day for Naranjo to return in order to kill him also. On March 12 Father Miranda wrote from Acoma to Governor Cubero that fifty Acoma warriors were ready and eager to leave for Zuñi and rescue Father Garaycoechea, but he was holding them back because the good padre had written that he would not leave his post without the permission of his major superior. Father Miranda also stated that Naranjo was especially anxious to go himself, but in his letter the priest of Zuñi had written that the Zuñi had laid ambushes for him along the way, and so he held him back also.[61] With Governor Vargas' return to Santa Fe for a second term, Naranjo must have been summoned to his side, for we find him as captain of Indian spies or scouts at Bernalillo in 1704, during the fateful Apache campaign when Vargas took sick and died.[62] During Ulibarrí's famed journey to El Cuartelejo in 1706, Naranjo headed a hundred Indians from every pueblo and did yeoman service as a guide and in contacts with the Apache chieftains. He discovered a needed water-spring which thereafter bore his name, Ojo de Naranjo, and he managed to have the Apache release the Picuris and let them return to their pueblo.[63]

In 1707 he was residing at Santa Cruz, where his good friend Roque de Madrid was still Alcalde Mayor of the villa. His name is the sixteenth on the list of the villagers, married to Catalina, with a family of seven persons.[64]

This Catalina was the bastard daughter of a certain Matías Luján of Santa Cruz. Naranjo also owned lands across the Rio Grande at La Vega (present Española), south of those belonging to an Antonio Salazar. These most likely were the ancestral lands which he inherited *in toto* after the death of his rebel brother Lucas. Of his several children, we know the name of his eldest son and heir, José Antonio Naranjo.[65]

In February 1709, after the Navajo stole some livestock from the Santa Clara side of the river, Naranjo and a captain went alone and followed their trail, and Governor Chacón sent out a troop to help the brave men.[66] In October 1713 the Navajo raided the livestock of San Ildefonso, and Governor Mogollón dispatched a troop of seventy Spaniards and one hundred fifty pueblo auxiliaries, Naranjo in full command of the latter.[67] Again, in 1715 Naranjo led the auxiliaries in another Navajo campaign.[68] As a permanent seal or symbol for all these activities, his name is found carved on Inscription Rock.[69]

Joseph subsequently appears, and still most active, in the two military documents of 1719 and 1720, already referred to in connection with the titles obtained from the Viceroy.[70] In the first, Governor Valverde conferred with his Spanish captains, and Naranjo also, on the advisability of waging a campaign against the Ute. Naranjo, still a resident of Santa Cruz, gave his reasons for attacking them. In the second, the same Governor asked his officers' opinions on the Viceroy's idea of establishing a garrison of twenty-five men and their families at El Cuartelejo, with friars to evangelize the gentile Indians. Here Naranjo gave the first "parecer," demonstrating the impracticality of such a plan, and all the Spanish officers seconded his opinion. This is the last we hear of him. But he must have lived on for many years, long enough to be remembered by some witnesses in 1766 as a black-complexioned individual with the soubriquets of "el Negro" and "el Mulato."

Fourth Generation: José Antonio Naranjo I. One witness of 1766 stated that he was somewhat lighter in complexion that his father Joseph, but did not know for sure if father and son were mulattoes or Indians; they had lived next to the pueblo of Santa Clara. Another flatly stated that José Antonio was an Indian from Santa Clara. Governor Cachupín then declared that, following the death of his father Joseph, José Antonio had moved to Santa Fe and received his title of War-Captain from Viceroy Revilla Gigedo.[71] This means that José Antonio, as the eldest son, had left the household in Santa Cruz to take care of the ancestral lands north of Santa Clara. Then, after his father's death, he went to Santa Fe in order to engage in the politics necessary to have his father's title conferred upon himself. José Antonio had married Juana Márquez de Ayala, of the colonists brought from Zacatecas by Vargas. Their eldest son was likewise named José Antonio (II), and they had a daughter Catalina, the wife of Salvador de Torres. Another son of theirs was most likely a Gerónimo Naranjo who married María Trujillo in 1743, and for whom Salvador de Torres and Catalina Naranjo stood as witnesses. Possibly another son, or perhaps a brother, was a Matías Naranjo, living in the same Santa Clara district with his wife María Varela. In 1731 José Antonio Naranjo had murdered a man and fled the kingdom.[72]

Fifth Generation: José Antonio Naranjo II, the man who in 1766 caused such a furor by wanting to be the field commander of Spanish troops as well as Indian. In 1747 he had gone all the way to Mexico City, and without permission. There he wangled an interview with the Viceroy himself to present the documents that compose this case. Apparently the Viceroy believed his story about his being descended from an original Spanish Conquistador of New Mexico, and about his direct ancestors all the way back having held the title of general commander of all colonial troops in the field. For in January 1748 the Marqués de las Amarillas conferred on him the title of "Capitán Mayor de la Gente de Guerra, en la villa de Santa Fe," in the place of his father José Antonio Naranjo (I). Later, Governor Marín del Valle (1754–1760) had angrily suspended the title because of gross disobedience and other charges. But after Vélez Cachupín came as Governor (1762–1767), Naranjo began working for his reinstatement. He got a glowing writ of commendation from Fray Juan José de Toledo, and his henchman Cristóbal Vigil gathered an impressive batch of signatures in his favor. First, Cachupín assigned him to the valley and pueblo of Taos with the "honorific title of Capitán y Justicia Mayor." Later, he apprised the militia of his intention of reinstating Naranjo according to the tenor of the documents which he presented.[73] This is what started the alarm among the Spanish officers and men and prompted Cachupín to look into the governmental archives in Santa Fe. As was mentioned before in connection with his father and grandfather, some thought he was a pure Tewa from Santa Clara while others declared that his forebears were a mixture of Negro and Indian. His title, if legitimate, was as war-captain for Indians only. Besides not being an "español," he was utterly incapable of exercising any military command for many serious reasons. For one thing, he was a notorious horse thief and cattle rustler. His no-good son, José, had recently murdered the son of Roque Jaramillo of Santa Cruz with bow and arrows.[74] The details of his rascality run into many pages, but are here passed over since they contribute nothing to the Naranjo family relationships and their connection with the Representative of Pohé-yemo.

Governor Cachupín's judgment was final. "All this proves that the title conferred on the present José Antonio Naranjo must be understood as *Capitán Mayor*, not of Spaniards, but of Indians (which was the one that his father and grandfather held). . . . Concerning the other Naranjos, whom Vargas found in the year ninety-three, and one of them was the already mentioned first Captain [Joseph Naranjo], their [racial] quality is not specified in the documents of that archive. The witnesses say, almost all, that they knew the grandfather of José Antonio Naranjo. And he, according to their testimonies, turns out to be a *Lobo, ó Mulato, ó Indio.* And what is certain is that, after the defect of his *calidad* had been set forth by the militia officials, he did not dare deny it. . . ."[75] In short, the results of the investigation were sent to Mexico City, and the Viceroy stripped Naranjo of his titles, ordering the local authorities to punish him and his companions in crime according to their deserts.[76]

It is of interest to note that in one of these papers Naranjo employs his mother's family name, Márquez de Ayala. His wife was Manuela Armenta, whom he had married in Santa Fe in 1749. She, like his mother, belonged to the colonists from Zacatecas. Other activities recorded about him, in addition to the case we have been treating, were a land transfer in 1752, a trial in 1756 for mistreating his Armenta wife, and other charges for assault in 1758.[77] These, and the entire episode of 1766, sadly demonstrate how much the main line of the vigorous and gifted black Naranjo family had fallen from the bizarre genius displayed by the great-grandfather in the Revolt of 1680, and from the enviable heights of achievement reached by the grandfather, Joseph López Naranjo, at the turn of the century.

3. Conclusion

That the famous Pueblo Revolt of 1680 was successfully planned and carried out, not alone by individual ritual leaders of each pueblo, but by a very real Representative of Pohé-yemo — a tall black man with big yellow eyes by the name of Naranjo — is amply demonstrated, I believe, by all the foregoing evidence. Whether or not Domingo Naranjo and Pedro Naranjo were one and the same man remains a moot question, although I incline toward the belief that they were brothers: Domingo the Representative of Pohé-yemo in Taos, and Pedro carrying out his orders at San Felipe. If Governor Otermín so officiously failed to recognize the chief culprit under his clever disguise, the basic truth did survive, even if in a confused way, in the long memory of the common Hispanic folk, as shown in the testimonies of 1766. It also had been preserved, although in a more legendary manner, in the tradition of Nuestra Señora de la Macana, in which the Devil himself is said to have appeared in the form of a black giant during the 1680 siege of Santa Fe.[78]

We can close this study most appropriately with a pueblo folktale about Pohé-yemo which was still being told in Santo Domingo not too long ago.

Because the story concerns an "ancient one" who in latter times is but a minor being among the *kopershtaya* or fetishes of the Indians, it must go back to those faraway times when the Person of Pohé-yemo had been greatly magnified and emphasized for the moment. And because the tale's form and flavor is not characteristic of the Indian genre of storytelling, but rather of the Spanish picaresque story, it could well have been composed just before the Revolt of 1680 by Naranjo himself and disseminated among the pueblos. The use of the form *Poshaiyanyi* for Pohé-yemo suggests that it came back to Santo Domingo by way of Zuñi:

> God and Poshaiyanyi were going to have a contest to see which one had the most power. They were going to shoot at a tree. God shot at it with a gun and cut a gash in the bark. Poshaiyanyi struck it with a bolt of lightning and split the trunk in half. Next they were going to see which one had the best things to eat. God had a table with lots of good things on it. Poshaiyanyi ate on the ground; he had some fat deer meat and some tortillas. God watched Poshaiyanyi eat for a while, then he got down on the ground and ate with him.
>
> Then they were going to see who could get some water from Shipap first. God wrote a letter. Poshaiyanyi made a wabani (feather bunch). He got water while someone was reading God's letter.
>
> The next was to see who could make the best music. God had a horn and blew on it. Poshaiyanyi used a drum and sang. After a while God got tired and gave up. God went home on a cloud; Poshaiyanyi left on the back of a duck.
>
> The next day they met again. They were going to shoot again. They shot at a rock this time. They decided to bet on the outcome. God bet some horses, cows, sheep, and one daughter. Poshaiyanyi bet corn and watermelons. God shot first; he just made a little nick in the rock. Poshaiyanyi struck it with a bolt of lightning and shattered it into bits. So Poshaiyanyi won again. He took the girl and started to go home. God got mad and sent some soldiers after him. But Poshaiyanyi got on a duck's back and went away to Wenima.[79]
>
> Before he left he told the Indians that there wouldn't be any more war between the Indians and anyone. If there were he would come back. He would gather all the Indians in one place and separate the good people from the witches. Then the earth will crack. Then everything will be new again — "when a mule has a baby."[80]

Notes

1. A general idea of these dissensions can be gathered throughout France V. Scholes, *Church and State in New Mexico, 1610–1650* (Albuquerque, 1937; also in the *New Mexico Historical Review* (hereafter NMHR), vol. 11, 1936, nos. 1–4; vol. 12, 1937, no. 1) and *Troublous Times in New Mexico, 1659–1670* (Albuquerque, 1942; also

in NMHR, vol. 12, 1937, nos. 2, 4; vol. 13, 1938, no. 1; vol. 15, 1940, nos. 3–4; vol. 16, 1941, nos. 1–3).

2. The pueblo religio-civic government was and is in the hands of two main groups: (1) the *Head Representatives* (representing both the people and the "ancient ones" in their mythology) which consist of the Chief Representative (cacique), the two War-Chieftains and their assistants, and the Heads of the kiva groups; (2) the *Medicinemen*, or Heads of the various curing societies and their assistants. Bandelier divided them into three: Warriors, Medicinemen, and the highest Shamans. And what jealousy between the caciques and the shamans, and what rivalry between the *Yaya* (cacique) and the war captains! Adolph F. Bandelier, *Final Report of Investigations among the Indians of the Southwestern United States,* 2 parts (Cambridge, 1890, 1892), part 1, pp. 148, 294. He refers in a note to Fray Alonso Benavides, who made two distinctions: *guerreros* and *hechiceros* (warriors and sorcerers, or medicinemen), who struggled against each other for dominion over the common people, and thus were the cause of internal and inter-tribal dissensions by which whole pueblos were laid desolate. Ibid., part 1, p. 148n.

3. Charles W. Hackett and Charmion C. Shelby, *Revolt of the Pueblo Indians of New Mexico and Otermín's Attempted Reconquest, 1680–1682,* 2 vols. (Albuquerque, 1942), vol. 1, p. 5. Italics mine.

4. Ibid., pp. 15–16. Italics mine. The introduction of a deified Montezuma, the Aztec Emperor, already points to a non-pueblo Indian behind the message.

5. Father Vélez Escalante in his extracts of the Otermín journals: "That they as youths were totally ignorant of the motive, and only had heard it said that from very far away toward the north there had come an order from an Indian *teniente* of Pojéyemú for all of this kingdom to rise against the Spaniards . . . that the *teniente* of Pojéyemú was very tall, black, and with eyes big and yellow." Biblioteca Nacional, México (cited hereinafter as BNM), leg. 3, no. 1 (20/428), Eleanor B. Adams transcript. He is the only source who aspirates the "h" and accents syllables. I am using the form and spelling "Pohé-yemo" as a compromise between old Spanish sources and the recordings of latter-day ethnologists.

6. The documents on the subject fill most of one volume: Archivo General de la Nación, Mexico (cited hereinafter as AGN), Tierras: Civil, tomo 426.

7. This I used, with other supporting documents, in an article, "Nuestra Señora de la Macana," NMHR, vol. 34 (1959), pp. 81–97. The idea was expanded into a "novel," both plot and characters taken entirely from the historical sources, entitled *The Lady from Toledo* (Fresno, 1960). Faulty deductions regarding the Representative of Pohé-yemo are corrected in this present study.

8. The Negro Estevanico certainly played with Fray Marcos de Niza's high hopes and gullibility on the way to Cibola in 1539. The martyrdom of Fray Pablo de Acevedo in Sinaloa in 1561 was attributed to a mulatto interpreter who twisted his words. Even in this very year of 1680, a rebellion planned by the Indians south of Guadalupe del Paso was blamed on the insensate actions of a mulatto servant, Hackett and Shelby, vol. 1, p. 47. For the escapades of an African native before and after the Vargas Reconquest, see my article, "De Vargas' Negro Drummer," *El Palacio,* vol. 56 (1949), pp. 131–38.

9. This synthesis of pueblo beliefs is gleaned from outstanding ethnologists: Bandelier, *Final Report,* and *The Southwest Journals of Adolph F. Bandelier, 1880–1882,* edited by Charles H. Lange and Carroll H. Riley (Albuquerque and Santa Fe, 1966); Noel Dumarest, *Notes on Cochiti, New Mexico,* edited by E. C. Parsons (Lancaster, Pa.,

1920); Elsie Clews Parsons, *The Pueblo of Jemez* (New Haven, 1925); Leslie A. White, *The Pueblo of San Felipe* (Menasha, Wis., 1932) and *The Pueblo of Santo Domingo* (Menasha, 1935); Charles H. Lange, *Cochiti* (Austin, 1959). My own observations and philosophical interpretation lead me to believe that there is no parallel here with the ancient deity religions of Asia Minor and Egypt, of Graeco-Roman mythology, or that of Aztec Mexico, much less with Judaeo-Christian religious concepts. Hence I studiously avoid any such confusing terminology as God, gods, spirit, worship, altar, priest, penitent, prayer, and the like. They have no relation to pure pueblo belief as such, even if the Indian himself, after early contact with Spanish Catholicity and now with the modern white man's parlance, has adopted such terms as Great Spirit, rain-gods, prayer sticks, etc.

10. Here I am using Keres terminology. The mythology is basically the same in all the pueblos, with local variations as to words and particular functions. The names vary according to language or dialect, even in their specific meaning, but there is always a general similarity in function and even nomenclature, for one linguistic group evidently borrowed from another, and vice versa. Since the tradition was entirely oral, it also suffered variation in neighboring pueblos of the same linguistic group. As ethnologists point out, the informants from each particular pueblo had confused ideas as to the exact nature and function of the "ancient ones."

11. Hackett and Shelby, vol. 1, p. 61.

12. Ibid., pp. 233–35.

13. Ibid., p. 295. Note the Spanish interpretation of the "sun-father" Pohé-yemo, who made the sun shine when the people came out of Shipapu.

14. Ibid., pp. 345, 361.

15. Ibid., pp. 117, 120, 122, 177, 194. The Indians who did the most harm were those who had been most favored by the friars, and were the most intelligent, wrote Fray Antonio de Sierra, ibid., p. 59.

16. AGN, Tierras: Civil, t. 426.

17. Ibid., II B, fol. 8.

18. George P. Hammond and Agapito Rey, *Don Juan de Oñate, Colonizer of New Mexico, 1595–1628* (Albuquerque, 1953), part 1, pp. 559, 562–63.

19. Ibid., pp. 155, 227, 233, 267, 299.

20. Ibid., pp. 146, 267. In the index the editors fail to distinguish fully between Alonso Naranjo, a native of Valladolid, pp. 164, 292, who did not remain in New Mexico, and *Alonso Martines* or *Martín* or *Martín Naranjo,* a native of Estremadura. The latter's son was undoubtedly the Diego Martines Naranjo killed by the Jemez around 1640–1645, Hackett and Shelby, vol. 2, p. 266. Perhaps also a Bartolo Martín (?) Naranjo. See note 67, infra. It is quite possible that this Spanish or part-Spanish family passed down as *Martín Barba,* for there are no Spaniards named Naranjo for the remainder of the century. See my book, *Origins of New Mexico Families in the Spanish Colonial Period* (cited hereinafter as NMF) (Santa Fe, 1954), pp. 71, 221.

21. Hammond and Rey, part 2, p. 561.

22. Ibid., pp. 559, 563.

23. AGN, Tierras: Civil, t. 426, II A, fol. 2.

24. Ibid., II B, fol. 8. There were no Spanish Naranjos at all in the Otermín refugee lists of 1680–1681, save possibly the Martín Barba family. The only man of this name was Pascual Naranjo, a mulatto of the Analco ward in Santa Fe, about whom more later.

25. Hackett and Shelby, vol. 2, pp. 211–12. Referring to the archives in 1766, Gov. Cachupín stated that "in the entry which Otermino made around the year

eighty-three [*sic*] . . . he arrested in the pueblo . . . of La Isleta, an Indian called Naranjo." AGN, Tierras: Civil, t. 426, III, fols. 74–75.

26. Hackett and Shelby, vol. 2, pp. 245–49. Father Vélez Escalante simply mentions an Indian called Pedro Naranjo, a great idolator and sorcerer, who had come from the upper pueblos to Isleta, sent there by the rebel leaders, BNM, leg. 3, no. 1 (20/428). In his written opinion, December 23, 1681, Fray Francisco de Ayeta said: "He is under arrest in this camp, is eighty years of age, and is a consummate sorcerer, and as such is noted and highly esteemed among them, as is proven by his having been found in La Isleta, teaching the diabolical manner and circumstances in which they must dance in their infamous and most obscene juntas (which they call cazinas). . . ." Hackett and Shelby, vol. 2, pp. 308–09. Father Ayeta goes on to relate all that Naranjo divulged to Otermín, but ends by attributing the Revolt to El Popé. But an Indian captive, Juan of Tesuque, declared that the rebel leaders had arranged for the destruction of the Isleta people, and that Naranjo had come down for this purpose. Ibid., pp. 329–30.

27. One Spaniard recalled how Gov. Argüello (1640, 1645) hanged 29 Jemez Indians for allying themselves with the Apache for a rebellion, and imprisoned others for killing a certain Diego Martines Naranjo. Another said he hanged more than forty. They claimed that Gov. Concha in 1650 discovered a plot by the Indians of Isleta, Alameda, San Felipe, Cochiti, and Jemez. They had agreed to turn loose all the Spaniards' horses, which were "the nerve of warfare," for the Apache to grab under pretense of a raid; then the pueblos would pounce on the Spaniards while they were assembled in prayer on Holy Thursday. As a result nine leaders were hanged and others sold as slaves for ten years. Then, under Gov. Villanueva (1664), six Piro of Senecú were hanged and others imprisoned for joining the Apache in an ambuscade that killed five Spaniards. Later, all the Piro pueblos of Las Salinas under Don Estéban Clemente "whom all the kingdom obeyed," plotted a general uprising, likewise planning to surprise the Spaniards on Holy Thursday. But the plot was discovered and this leader was hanged. Ibid., pp. 266, 299–300. Note the title and full name of Don Estéban Clemente; they stamp him as non-pueblo, another intelligent hybrid full of resentment against the Spaniard.

28. Communication by means of deerskin paintings is a Plains Indian feature. Perhaps the Taos acquired it from their close contact with them.

29. Francisco Xavier and Luis de Quintana, natives respectively of Sevilla and Balmaseda, and Diego López Sambrano, a native New Mexican of Santa Fe, were a trio whom the Indian ritual leaders hated the most. They were the officials who for the last five years under Governors Treviño and Otermín (1675–1680) had gone about destroying kivas and Indian shrines, and severely punishing the ritual leaders. Under Treviño they carried out a terrible witch-hunt occasioned by the complaints of the voluble and superstitious Fray Andrés Durán of San Ildefonso. Forty-seven Tewas were arrested for witchcraft, and four of them were hanged for alleged witchcraft and murder. Among the other prisoners taken to Santa Fe was El Popé himself. The aroused warriors of all the Tewa pueblos then confronted Treviño at the palace, and he released the prisoners. Ibid., pp. 300–301. When the leaders were asked why they rebelled, both by Otermín in 1681 and by Vargas in 1692–1693, they referred time and again to this hated trio. For their lives, see NMF, pp. 58, 89, 113.

30. In the previous year the Spanish clerk described the knotted cord as being made of thongs of animal hide. Perhaps the "timetable" sent to some other pueblos was on cords made of yucca fiber.

31. The Representative of Pohé-yemo at Taos, and therefore himself and/or

Domingo Naranjo. He certainly would not have himself identified and then be hanged like the Piro Estéban Clemente mentioned in note 27, supra.

32. *Degollados.* A purely Spanish form of execution. It was decapitation by first slitting the throat and then the entire neck.

33. The pueblos were strictly monogamous. Even if considerable liberty was allowed to the young, until conception took place for a pair, after marriage there was only one wife, and adultery was severely punished. The polygamy offered here is African and Aztec.

34. Pedro Naranjo's entire declaration is in Hackett and Shelby, vol. 2, pp. 245–49.

35. Naranjo says that the three spirits went underground, but then adds that one of them (*El Caudi*) remained to give orders with El Popé, and thus *El Caudi* suggests one of the names of the high priest of Tlascala, *Achcautli*. See Fray Gerónimo de Mendieta, *Historia Eclesiástica Indiana* (Mexico, 1870), lib. 2, cap. 7. When combined with the other two spirits, we have a resemblance to the gods *Omacatl* (two reed) and *Ixtlilton* (little black face) who was also called *Tlaltetecuini* (earth stamper). Or, more significantly, the names of the three spirits recall Fire worshipped as a god under the names: *Ixcoçauhqui, Cueçaltzin, Ueueteotl.* See Arthur J. O. Anderson and Charles E. Dibble, *Florentine Codex,* edition of Fray Bernardino de Sahagún (Santa Fe, 1950), Book I, *The Gods,* part 2, pp. 14–15, 39, 42. During the Fire Festivals honoring this god, the lords and consuls were elected, and "after these feasts, they forthwith proclaimed war against their foes." Ibid. It would be most natural for Naranjo to have an imperfect grasp of names in Aztec-Tlascaltec myth, as received from parents who themselves probably had a garbled memory of them.

36. Bandelier thought that "Copala" was a copyist's error for *Ci-bo-bé,* the Tewa word for *Shipapu. Final Report,* part 2, pp. 29–30. However, the original texts have *Copala,* and the context calls for it. Vélez Escalante places an accent on the last syllable, *Copalá.* The genesis of the Copala legend can be outlined as follows:

(1) Sixteenth-century writers related legends of the Toltecs, Aztecs, and Chichimecas, as how they had come down from the north in slow stages from a place called *Aztlan* or *Huehuetlalpallan* or *Tlalpallan.* One group on the way down lingered at a place called "Seven Caves." Different friars and colonists heard the story from different natives, and so the legend and the terminology varied, and more so with repetition.

(2) *Tlalpala* became identified, if incorrectly, with the place of the Seven Caves, and these with the "Seven Cities" of a Portuguese romance which the Spaniards of those times took for history. This is what led Fray Marcos de Niza to look for them in 1539 in the far north whence the Mexican nations had come. But he and Coronado in 1540 were sadly disappointed with the Seven Cities of Cibola, for the mud Zuñi villages had neither glamour nor gold. Yet the Spanish imagination would not give up. There had to be, somewhere in the *north,* that fabulous and rich place of the original inhabitants of Mexico, the birthplace of "*Montezuma,*" as the imperial name had become confused with those of the original leaders and gods of the Mexicans. Its fabled treasures made it *another* Mexico, a *new* Mexico, in the minds of adventurers.

(3) There was a town of *Copala* on the flanks of the Colima range, an area where rich mining operations were going on in the 1530's, and this could have helped confuse it with *Tlalpala.* At any rate, the fortune hunters by the middle of the century were referring to the northern home of the Mexicans as Copala, which Coronado

must have missed when he came upon Cibola. This prompted several forays into what is now northern Mexico, the chief of which was Ibarra's "quest of Copala." In 1563 he came upon a populous fertile valley, and reported that he had found the legendary Copala; the place was a disappointment, but the name stuck. In 1582 three friars and some soldiers reached the Rio Grande pueblos and said they had found "the *new* Mexico." Suddenly, the names of Copala and New Mexico became interchangeable. There was a lake into which the Rio Nazas emptied (near Ibarra's Copala), which was given the name "Lago de Nuevo Mexico," and this seems to be where Copala became a lake.

(4) Soon after New Mexico was colonized in 1598, the Lake of Copala became a "fact." In 1605 Oñate had made his famous trip in search of the South Sea and here, wrote Father Zárate Salmerón, "was the first news they had of the lake of Copalla, whence it is presumed the Mexicans came who settled New Spain." Oñate's men had asked the natives living near the mouth of the Colorado about this lake of Copala and they, like other natives before them and afterwards, pleased their visitors by describing such a fantastic lake and city toward the north. Thus it became the subject of fireside chats and dreams among the pioneer settlers of New Mexico — and among these were the first and second generations of the black Naranjos. Now a Naranjo was further confusing the legendary Copala with the Pueblo Indians' own mythical place of origin, the Hole of Shipapu. Bandelier and Cushing relate pueblo folktales in which the lake-idea of Copala and the hole-idea of Shipapu have become further confused, particularly among the Jémez and the Zuñi. Bandelier, *Final Report* part 2, pp. 29–30, 207, 587. But these are relatively modern accretions, not the original myth. Who knows but that they started around 1680?

37. AGN, Tierras: Civil, t. 426, II A, fol. 3. Here I am using the old forms "Joseph" and "Josephe" as found in the manuscripts (in those times pronounced "Josép" and "Josépe," hence the diminutive "Pepe") to distinguish him more easily from the others named "José" in the same narratives.

38. Ibid., II B, fol. 47.

39. Ibid., fol. 78.

40. Hackett and Shelby, vol. 2, p. 231. Juan of Tesuque, who blamed El Popé for the rebellion, had been an employed servant of Francisco Xavier, the nemesis of the ritual leaders and their kivas. Here it is mentioned that Xavier lost two mulatto slaves at Picuris. These were Francisco Blanco de la Vega, native of Puebla, and María Madrid or "La Mozonga," who was taken captive with her children and was later rescued by the Vargas forces in 1692. See NMF, p. 307, and "Rendón" in *El Palacio*, vol. 64 (May–June, 1957), pp. 180–81.

41. Joseph's entire testimony, Hackett and Shelby, vol. 2, pp. 238–42. Sebastián de Herrera Corrales had taken his family up to Taos on a visit, while he and Sargento Mayor Fernando de Chávez went further on to trade with the Ute. Both their families were wiped out by the Taos. On their return the two officers, and a Chávez youth who was with his father, saw what had happened and fled south past the besieged villa of Santa Fe, and caught up with the refugees of the Río Abajo. NMF, pp. 21–22, 47. Hence young Joseph must have accompanied Herrera to the Ute country and thus escaped south with him and the two Chávez men.

42. Hackett and Shelby, vol. 2, pp. 243–45. Yet, this Lucas might have been what he said, and not Josephe's brother. But strangely enough, Lucas Naranjo was tied in with some Piro Indians in the uprising of 1696.

43. Ibid., pp. 231–32, 249–53.

44. Ibid., vol. 1, p. 12. At the same time Otermín sent another trusted Indian, Juan el Tano, to see what his people were doing in Galisteo; but he returned as the leader of the Tano rebels. Ibid., pp. 12–14. I identify this Juan as the desecrator of the Macana image who was hanged by the Devil in the form of a black giant after having repented his sacrilege, for he fits in perfectly with the Macana legend. See notes 7, supra, and 78, infra.

45. On October 2, 1680, "Pascual Naranjo, mulatto, pitifully poor, passed muster on foot and without any arms, with a family of wife and six children. He did not sign because of not knowing how." Hackett and Shelby, vol. 1, p. 158. Pascual's wife was María Romero, nicknamed "Cota, la Naranja." This family, and practically all the Analco people, remained at Guadalupe del Paso instead of returning to Santa Fe in 1693. Two of their children married at Guadalupe del Paso in 1692 and 1698, NMF, p. 80. Most likely another son was the José Naranjo who testified for another former resident of Analco at Guadalupe del Paso in 1692. See note 50, infra. Earlier in the century Don Pedro de Chávez had equipped Pascual Naranjo with a cutlass and two horses during a campaign against the wild Indians, Hackett and Shelby, vol. 2, p. 177. Chávez' father, Don Pedro I, had owned a mulatto servant by the name of Diego de Santiago, whom he kept employed at his Rancho tel Tunque near San Felipe Pueblo in the 1630's. Diego's wife was Felipilla, most probably from the pueblo, AGN, Inquisición, t. 372, exp. 19, fols. 17–18v. My guess is that Diego de Santiago was a brother of Domingo and/or Pedro Naranjo, and that he and Felipilla were the parents of Pascual Naranjo of Analco and of the mulatto woman living at "the rancho near San Felipe," the mother of the slain Bartolomé Naranjo and his two half-brothers, the Lorenzo boys. Father Vélez Escalante is the only writer who refers to *Tlascaltecas* living in Analco before the Revolt. In 1680 there were eight Analco families designated as "Mexican Indians." Probably, like Pascual Naranjo, they also had Tlascaltec antecedents, in the other two daughters of Don Joseph de Tepeaca and other women in the Oñate lists. It is not impossible that the padre heard this from the descendants of Pascual Naranjo and other such folk, and so was prompted to make the statement.

46. Hackett and Shelby, vol. 2, pp. 362–63.

47. AGN, Historia, t. 37, no. 6, fols. 124 et seq.

48. In 1631 the young mestizo Gerónimo Pacheco (perhaps the father of this Francisco Pacheco) was a good friend of the young mulatto Diego de Santiago treated in note 45, supra. Father Vélez Escalante relates an interesting episode which seems to refer to this Francisco Pacheco. Treating of this submission of the Taos to Gov. Vargas, he mentions Pacheco, but not Josephillo, then goes on to relate this incident which he took from an authentic testimonial of March 1681. It was given at Guadalupe del Paso by Alonso Shimitihua, cousin of the rebel mestizo Alonso Catati of Santo Domingo. Gov. Otermín had sent Shimitihua with some other trusted Indians to confer with the rebels and persuade them to make peace. Some of his companions defected to the rebels, and he was made prisoner and taken to Taos. There he witnessed the desecration of a statue of the Virgin Mary together with some Spanish cadavers. This image had been discovered in the house of an Indian "mestizo" married to a Taos woman and nicknamed "el Portugués." Shimitihua later escaped and returned to tell the Spaniards of his adventures, BNM, leg. 3, no. 1 (20/428).

49. AGN, Historia, t. 37, no. 6. In the 1766 controversy, Gov. Cachupín stated, after consulting the archives, that Vargas in an early entrada found a mestizo (Pa-

checo) and one of those called Naranjo (Josephillo) at Taos. AGN, Tierras: Civil, t. 426, III, fol. 74v. But then Cachupín confused Josephillo with the Naranjo (Lucas) who led the Tewas, Picuris, and Taos in the Revolt of 1696. Ibid. He also said that Vargas made Joseph Naranjo his pet—"acaricó a Joseph Naranjo." Ibid., II B, fol. 8.

50. On January 19, 1692, a Joseph Naranjo at Guadalupe del Paso had testified that he was 22 years old and had known young Juan de León Brito all his life, for they were reared together, Archives of the Archdiocese of Santa Fe, Diligencias Matrimoniales, 1692, no. 3. The León Britos were also "Mexican Indians" from Analco in Santa Fe, hence this Joseph Naranjo must be a son of Pascula Naranjo. See note 46, supra.

51. AGN, Historia, t. 38, pt. 1, fol. 72; Vélez Escalante, BNM, leg. 3, no. 1 (20/428). Gov. Cachupín mistakenly identified him as Joseph Naranjo. Ibid.; Tierras: Civil, t. 426, III, fol. 74v.

52. Spanish Archives of New Mexico, State Records Center and Archives, Santa Fe (cited hereinafter as SANM), no. 60a; *Old Santa Fe,* vol. 3 (October 1916), p. 368.

53. Lucas was clearly implicated by the declarations of several witnesses, SANM, no. 60a; *Old Santa Fe,* vol. 3, pp. 359–65. "Su primer motor de este levantamiento nombrado Naranjo." AGN, Historia, t. 38, fols. 50–52.

54. AGN, Tierras: Civil, t. 426, II A, fol. 3; II B, fols. 8–8v. The witness was wrong concerning the last accusation, for the Cuartelejo episode took place many years later when Joseph Naranjo was already a trusted and sincere ally of the Spaniards. But it is evident that Naranjo had left an enviable reputation as a linguist.

55. Letter of Father Garaycoechea, Zuñi, May 28, 1700. Here the padre refers to him as Joseph López Naranjo. BNM, leg. 3, no. 1 (20/428).

56. This declaration and the certifications which follow are all written in the same clear hand, including all signatures with their rubrics. They are no doubt a copy of originals. Joseph's signature and rubric are obviously a deliberate sham by the copyist, for he could not sign his name in 1681, nor afterwards in his declarations of 1702, 1719, 1720. SANM, nos. 84, 301.

57. AGN, Tierras: Civil, t. 426, fols. 37–38. The year is thus written out for 1698, a mistake by the mid-eighteenth century copyist. Fray Agustín de Colina, in 1704, substantiates Naranjo's statement that he had indeed saved the lives of the padres when they went to the Hopi pueblos in 1700, BNM, leg. 5, no. 5, leg. 7, no. 1, fols. 42–43.

58. SANM, nos. 301, 308.

59. Bancroft Library, University of California, Berkeley, New Mexico Originals (cited hereinafter as NMO), 1702. In 1766 Gov. Cachupín stated from the archives that Joseph Naranjo had been useful to Vargas, who commissioned him in these enterprises to the extent of sending him to Zuñi and the Hopi pueblos, and naming him Major War-Captain of all the Indians "so that he might with greater authority be a part of the entire reduction." AGN, Tierras: Civil, t. 426, III, fols. 75–75v.

60. SANM, no. 84.

61. Vélez Escalante, BNM, leg, 3, no. 1 (20/428).

62. SANM, no. 99.

63. AGN, Provincias Internas, t. 36, pt. 4, fols. 359v–368.

64. Padrón de la Parroquia de Santa Cruz de los Españoles, 1707, BNM, leg. 6, no. 4 (25/487).

65. NMF, p. 241.

66. SANM, no. 154.

67. Ibid., no. 199.

68. NMO, 1715.

69. The name is carved in large letters, JOSEPH NARANJO, without any date. It bears no relation to a much later carving beneath it, of 1774. Photo reproductions in John M. Slater, *El Morro, Inscription Rock* (Los Angeles, 1961), plate 36, p. 93. It could have been carved for Naranjo by some literate companion when he traveled back and forth between Acoma and Zuñi as Alcalde Mayor of these two pueblos from 1700 to 1703; or else during the Ulibarrí campaigns of 1701 or 1709, when the latter left his inscriptions on the rock. Naranjo's name is about a hundred feet from them. There is another Naranjo signature next to an inscription of 1620: BAR-TOLOM NARANJO, with a rubric and a nick above the "M." Ibid., plate 83, p. 120. Slater and others have deciphered it as "Bartolome Naranjo." To me it looks rather like an abbreviated "Bartolo Martín Naranjo," hence possibly a literate individual of the early seventeenth century, perhaps another son of Alonso Martín Naranjo. Cf. note 20, supra.

70. SANM, nos. 301, 308.

71. AGN, Tierras: Civil, t. 426, II B, fols. 47, 49, 75v et seq.

72. NMF, p. 241.

73. AGN, Tierras: Civil, t. 426, II B, fols. 70v–74, 79v.

74. Ibid., fol. 2 et seq.

75. Ibid., fols. 76, 78.

76. Ibid., fols. 82–84.

77. NMF, pp. 241–42.

78. See note 7, supra. Gov. Vargas must have heard the Macana tradition of 1680 from the refugee colonists at Guadalupe del Paso, for, to heighten the drama of his own reconquest of Santa Fe in 1693, he referred to it in his official report as actually happening at this time. Vélez Escalante, BNM, leg. 3, no. 1 (20/428). This Macana tradition is entirely distinct from that of La Conquistadora. See my books on this particular Marian image, *Our Lady of the Conquest* (Santa Fe, 1948) and *La Conquistadora: The Autobiography of an Ancient Statue* (Paterson, N.J., 1954).

79. White, *Santo Domingo,* pp. 178–79. This seems to be the end of the original tale, in which God-Friar-Spaniard has been pitted against Pohé-yemo-Medicineman-Indian.

80. Ibid. This last paragraph is a confused reference to the Christian Last Judgment and Salvation, regarding which the Indian expresses his doubt by the last remark. But even this is a very old Spanish expression: "El día que pare la mula."

Andrew L. Knaut

Acculturation and Miscegenation: The Changing Face of the Spanish Presence in New Mexico

From *The Pueblo Revolt of 1680: Conquest and Resistance in Seventeenth-Century New Mexico*

The story of the Pueblo Revolt is usually told as an Indian struggle for survival against Spaniards. Andrew Knaut, in a book-length study of the revolt published in 1995, reminds us that the Hispanic and Pueblo worlds came together in many ways in the seventeenth century. "Pueblo and Spaniard found their lives woven together with increasing intricacy . . . altering the relationship of vassal to colonial overlord in the region," Knaut says in the preface to his book. He argues that the two societies did not divide or unite solely along the lines of race and culture. Pueblos quarreled with Pueblos and Spaniards with Spaniards. Nonetheless, Knaut maintains, Pueblos kept their culture intact and waited for the opportunity to overthrow their new masters.

In one of the most original chapters in his book, Knaut explains the specific ways in which divisions between the Pueblo and Spanish worlds blurred over the course of the seventeenth century. For Knaut, miscegenation and acculturation did not lead to harmony, however, but rather contributed to the Pueblos' successful revolt. Spaniards lost the ability to intimidate Pueblos. Pueblos, he tells us, learned enough about the weaknesses of their new Spanish masters to know how to get rid of them. In that sense, Knaut contradicts Chávez's argument that it took a non-Pueblo to lead the 1680 revolt. The Pueblos themselves, Knaut suggests, had ample knowledge.

Andrew Knaut's interest in the Pueblo Revolt grew out of his southwestern upbringing and his training in colonial Latin American history. A native of El Paso, he completed a combined M.D.-Ph.D. program at Duke University in 1995. Colonial Latin America was his historical specialty, and his dissertation on Bourbon efforts to implement public health measures in New Spain's Atlantic ports brought his interests together. He is currently completing an internship in emergency medicine in Denver.

Questions for a Closer Reading

1. What kind of evidence does Knaut offer to demonstrate that cultural boundaries blurred between Pueblos and Spaniards?

2. How does Knaut know that Spaniards borrowed "magic" from the Pueblos and not from Spanish folk religion?

3. What kind of evidence does Knaut offer to demonstrate racial mixture between Spaniards and Pueblos?

4. How does Knaut know that Spaniards—a category that included *mestizos,* mulattoes, and other mixed bloods— had sexual relations with Pueblo Indians?

5. Why does Knaut focus almost exclusively on ways that Spaniards adopted Pueblo traits over ways that Pueblos adopted Spanish traits?

Acculturation and Miscegenation: The Changing Face of the Spanish Presence in New Mexico

New Mexico and its native inhabitants together exerted a profound influence upon the handful of Hispanics who called the territory home in the seventeenth century. The land made life hard on those unable to withstand its furies, breaking some and bending others to a shape and appearance as rugged as the terrain itself. Pueblo culture, with a tradition and a social order dating back centuries, resisted Spanish efforts toward a guided change of its values, beliefs, and ideals. Immersed in this culture, Hispanic colonists could not escape adopting many of its aspects. Pueblo ways, so foreign and so savage to the original colonists in the closing years of the sixteenth century, became second nature to subsequent generations of settlers. Over the course of the seventeenth century, the forces of nature and acculturation combined to bury Oñate's vision of Spanish domination through cultural separation and superiority. In time, the faces of the Hispanic settlers changed so markedly that they would have been unrecognizable to their predecessors in the ranks of Oñate's followers.

In 1598, Captain Luis Gasco de Velasco had presented himself for the conquest of New Mexico, a man twenty-eight years old, crimson bearded and of medium stature, and a native of Cuenca, Spain.[1] An inventory of his possessions to be taken on the expedition northward revealed personal effects of a decidedly European sort:

> First, he exhibited and brought before his lordship a standard of figured white Castilian silk, with fringes and trimmings of gold and crimson silk. . . .
> Item: A silver lance, in its handle, for the exercise of his office as captain, with tassels of gold and yellow and purple silk.

Andrew L. Knaut, "Acculturation and Miscegenation: The Changing Face of the Spanish Presence in New Mexico," in *The Pueblo Revolt of 1680: Conquest and Resistance in Seventeenth-Century New Mexico* (Norman: University of Oklahoma Press, 1995), 136–51.

Item: Three sets of horse armor of buckskin, lined with undressed leather, for the flanks, foreheads, breasts, necks—all, without anything lacking.

Item: A sword and a gilded dagger with their waist belts stitched with purple, yellow, and white silk.

Item: One bed with two mattresses, a coverlet, sheets, pillow-cases, pillows, and a canvas mattress-bag bound with leather. . . .

Item: One suit of blue Italian velvet trimmed with wide gold pasementerie, consisting of doublet, breeches, and green silk stockings with blue garters with points of gold lace. . . .

Item: Another suit of Chinese flowered silk. . . .

Item: Eight pairs of Cordovan leather boots, six white pairs, and four black, and four pairs of laced gaiters.

Item: Two hats, one black, trimmed around the crown with a silver cord, with black, purple, and white feathers and the other gray, with yellow and purple feathers.[2]

The complete list filled three pages of text.

Sixty-five years later, an immense cultural and genetic gap had emerged to separate Velasco from his counterpart in a drastically changed New Mexican Hispanic society of the 1660s. Nicolás de Aguilar, at various times holder of the offices of field captain, sergeant, and adjutant in the villa of Santa Fe and alcalde mayor of the district Las Salinas, stood before the tribunal of the Inquisition in Mexico City on April 12, 1663. His examiners described him as a thirty-six-year-old man "of large body, coarse and somewhat brown," a mestizo, a reputed murderer, and an accused heretic.[3] Dressed in flannel trousers and woolen shirt and stockings—all crudely woven and in places badly frayed—and wearing a cotton neckcloth and buckskin shoes of the type commonly worn by colonists in New Mexico, Aguilar handed his inquisitors the key to a small wooden box that had accompanied him on his journey from the northern province. The box contained all of the accused's possessions, collected in New Mexico and sent south by commissary Posadas for closer scrutiny by his superiors in the Holy Office in the viceregal capital. Upon opening it, Aguilar's examiners found only a collection of well-worn clothing and a few personal items that included

3. A doublet of buff and black wool, badly worn, with cotton sleeves embroidered with blue wool. . . .

5. Item. An old cotton shirt, adorned with drawn work.

6. Item. Another cloth shirt, worn out. . . .

12. One pair of shoes of Córdovan leather, worn out.

13. A book, entitled, "Catechism in the Castilian and Timuquana languages." Inside of this was another very small book, entitled, "Instructions for examining the conscience."

14. A bar of soap and a little *alucema* wrapped in an old black rag.

15. An antelope skin muffler lined with yellow linen.

16. A cloth containing, apparently, roots of dry grass, which he said they call bear grass in New Mexico, used for curing fevers.

17. Three small pieces of dried grass roots, which he said is called *manso* grass, and is good for healing wounds. . . .

21. A rosary strung on *coyole* wire, having large beads, and a little silver cross. . . .

25. A buckskin bag within which is a cotton pillow filled with sheep's wool.

26. A mattress of coarse black and white stuff, filled with sheep's wool.[4]

As a mestizo, Aguilar represented what had become, by the time of his birth in the third decade of the seventeenth century, a large proportion of the Hispanic population in the province. Isolated among an overwhelming native population, Hispanics in New Mexico inevitably intermixed with Pueblo Indians. Even before the mass desertion of the colony in 1601, only forty-two of the region's two hundred male Spaniards had brought families with them from the south.[5] No quantitative data exist, but surviving documentary evidence indicates that Pueblo and Spanish ancestries blended at a rate sufficient to alarm those conservative members of the colony who were convinced of the need to maintain clear lines of European heritage in the midst of a Pueblo majority.

Pointing to the results of more than a generation of miscegenation within the province, Fray Esteban de Perea, commissary of the Holy Office in New Mexico at that time, lamented in 1631 that in presiding over the duties of the Inquisition he was forced to deal with a population that contained "so many *mestizos, mulattos,* and bastards, and others [who are] worse . . . and of [such] little moral strength that I am sometimes confused [by their testimonies in these investigations]."[6] Three decades later, Inquisition officials attempted to deflate Governor Peñalosa's air of self-importance during the latter's appearance before the tribunal by reminding him that "he was merely the governor and captain general of fifty men, [composed] of the dregs of the earth, *mestizos* and mulattoes."[7]

Further evidence of widespread miscegenation in the colony lies in the fact that as the century progressed many mestizos and others of mixed racial background attained official positions in New Mexico's colonial government, a rare phenomenon in other parts of a rigidly caste-oriented Spanish-American empire.[8] No development reflects more accurately the scarcity of Spanish "pure-bloods" to fill vital posts in New Mexico. During Rosas's administration, one friar objected to the governor's manipulation of the elections for the 1639–41 cabildo and referred to the men who eventually won seats on the council as "those four *mestizo* dogs."[9] Decades later, the ranks of officials of mixed heritage included not only Nicolás de Aguilar but also Captain Francisco de Ortega, listed in 1669 as a mulatto;[10] Juan Luján, in 1665 the alcalde mayor of Los Taos and a *mestizo amulatado;*[11] Joseph Nieto, in 1667 the mulatto alcalde mayor of Las Salinas;[12] and Alonso García, lieutenant governor of New Mexico in 1680, head official of Spanish colonial authority for the entire Río Abajo region, and a mestizo.[13]

The destabilizing effect of such a large mestizo population among the colonials in New Mexico cannot be overemphasized. Looked down upon by Hispanics of pure blood as "half-breeds" and yet in many cases expected to fill roles of responsibility in the colony, mestizos found themselves pushed in different directions by the deep-seated ambivalence prevalent among the Spanish settlers. Such social pressures could prove explosive and gave rise to frequent incidents of violence and confrontation. In 1639, Diego Martín, a mestizo, led an uprising in the pueblo of Taos that resulted in the deaths of the Franciscan friar in residence and two soldiers.[14] During Governor López de Mendizábal's administration (1659–62) and his legalization of the kachinas, many friars feared the role that mestizos might take in the turmoil generated by the Pueblo cultural revival. Fray Alonso de Posadas expressed concern over the effect that such an atmosphere would have, "especially [on] those of low degree, such as *mestizos.*"[15]

Nicolás de Aguilar only confirmed the Franciscan's fears. Upon his excommunication by custodian García de San Francisco in 1660, the mestizo simply rose "from the place where he was, putting on his hat and turning his back, [and] replied to the judge that he did not care for all the excommunications in the world."[16] Frustrated, San Francisco resigned his duties as ecclesiastical judge, "saying that he did not wish to proceed with people who had no fear of God or of censures."[17] Emblematic of a Hispanic society that had forsaken its distance from the surrounding Pueblo populace, New Mexico's mestizo presence could not be ignored.

At the same time, many mestizos capitalized on their poorly defined status in seventeenth-century New Mexico, moving extensively—if often clandestinely—within both Pueblo and Hispanic social circles.[18] In doing so, these "crossovers" served as important intermediaries in a process of acculturation that over the course of the century slowly blurred the lines differentiating European newcomer from Pueblo Indian. But mestizos were only one of many vectors by which Pueblo culture penetrated the Hispanic community. The colonists' isolation from events transpiring to the south and their numerically small presence in a land where the indigenous inhabitants numbered in the tens of thousands meant that everyday contacts between Hispanic settlers and Pueblo Indians were as extensive as they were inevitable. Openings for settlers to learn of and accept Pueblo ways proved ubiquitous. As time wore on and as the newcomers seized these opportunities to gain from Pueblo convention and experience, important changes transpired in the life-style of New Mexico's colonists.

Hispanic exposure to the Pueblos—their style of living, their attitudes and beliefs, their folk practices—began in childhood. In the schools of religious instruction run by the friars, Hispanic and Pueblo boys learned together, sang together, and, presumably, played together, in many ways closing the gap that separated their parents' worlds.[19] Apparently this process began almost as soon as Oñate's original colonists entered the region. As early as 1601, Ginés de Herrera Horta told of meeting in New Mexico "a Spanish boy, who, as the lad himself told him, grew up among the Indian boys. He knew the language of the Picurís or Queres better than the Indians themselves, and they were astonished to hear him talk."[20] Several decades later, this first generation of New Mexico–raised Hispanics reached adulthood and assumed roles of leadership within the colony, causing Fray Esteban de Perea to complain in 1628 of conditions "in this new land and among this people, raised from childhood with the customs of these Indians, with neither decency nor schools . . . who blossom out as captains and royal officials."[21]

Certainly one of the major factors that pushed Hispanic settlers into accepting Pueblo practices was the extremely limited availability of medical care in the European sense of the term. No institutionally trained and licensed physicians or surgeons practiced in the northern province during the seventeenth century. Instead, the filling of this niche fell to those members of the colony who generally boasted the highest level of formal education—the Franciscan missionaries. Very little has survived to illuminate the manner in which the friars carried out this charge in the missions and throughout the Hispanic community, but it is evident that the church did attach importance to caring for its followers during times of sickness. By 1631 the Franciscans had established an infirmary for the colony that, documentary evidence suggests, was located in the mission at San Felipe.[22] The arrival of the triennial caravan brought with it supplies for that infirmary: linens, medicinal herbs and preserves, and a few basic surgical instruments.[23] In addition, each pair of friars serving in the missionary field received a copper cupping instrument, one syringe, a razor, one lancet, and a pair of barber scissors, indicating that bloodletting and other minor invasive procedures were practiced with some frequency in the missions.[24]

Still, it is doubtful whether care at the hands of the friars was a practical or even an attractive option for the majority of those Hispanics stricken with illness in New Mexico during the seventeenth century. Thirty miles separated the most important European settlement at Santa Fe from the infirmary at San Felipe, making access to that facility impractical for most colonists. Throughout the province, the small number of friars and their wide geographic dispersion meant long traveling distances for those needing medical attention but not living in the shadow of a mission with a friar in residence. Logistical problems aside, it is not hard to imagine the reluctance with which many settlers viewed the prospect of submitting to therapy at the end of a razor wielded by a priest with little or no formal medical training.

These factors combined with the constant interaction between Hispanic settlers and the surrounding Pueblo majority to make indigenous folk medicine and *curanderismo* the preferred options for relief from illness, facilitating the process by which Pueblo ways gained acceptance and permeated the European community. In addition to documenting Aguilar's possession of bear grass (used, apparently, for curing fevers) and manso grass for healing wounds, Inquisition testimonies from this period reveal many examples of Hispanic settlers in New Mexico turning to Pueblo Indians in search of medicines, aphrodisiacs, and love potions.

Franciscans in seventeenth-century New Mexico recognized as well as any cultural anthropologist or ethnohistorian working among twentieth-century Pueblo communities that native medicinal practices intertwined tightly with Pueblo cosmology and worldviews. Dismayed references to Hispanic settlers' having resorted to Pueblo cure-alls appear with impressive frequency in the Inquisition documents from the period. Charges of nativism and "sorcery" leveled against a colonist often spurred the commissary of the Holy Office to embark on lengthy inquiries into the accused's private affairs. Something of the flavor of daily life in New Mexico's Hispanic community has been preserved in the testimonies generated by these investigations. At the same time, the documents provide an invaluable glimpse into the manner in which members of the European population opened themselves to an acceptance of Pueblo ways.

One illustrative example of this cultural transmission from Pueblo to Hispanic society is that of Beatriz de los Angeles. A mestiza and the widow of alférez Juan de la Cruz, de los Angeles lived on an estancia amid the Tano pueblos southwest of Santa Fe. Throughout the 1620s, she enjoyed a reputation among the Hispanic community as a "sorceress of compassion" or, more clearly, a *curandera* who proffered home remedies and incantations from the vantage point of one who moved in both Indian and European circles.[25] Supporters recounted the tale of how de los Angeles traveled to Senecú in 1628 to help doña María Granillo overcome a serious illness. There, while in the company of "other witches," the curandera apparently saved her patient's life by playing patoles with Granillo and simultaneously reciting a number of spells.[26]

But de los Angeles's reputed talents included more than the ability to cure illness through shamanism. For years, women in the Hispanic community had sought her help in curbing the amorous pursuits of wayward husbands. Usually, de los Angeles answered these requests by prescribing *gusanos ciegos,* a type of worm gathered easily in any dung heap in the region, and directing her clients to hide them in the food eaten by the men in question.[27] Problems arose for de los Angeles, however, at the close of the decade when she gave this concoction to her own partner, Diego Bellido. Bellido grew violently ill upon ingesting a bowl of milk laced with the worms, and when de los Angeles attempted to nullify the potion by giving Bellido an unspecified oil as an emetic, his condition only worsened, leading ultimately to his death.[28] The incident drew the attention of commissary Estevan de Perea and generated a lengthy investigation by the Inquisition into de los Angeles's activities.

Numerous examples also survive of colonial settlers approaching Pueblo Indians directly in search of folk remedies. To the dismay of inquisitors like Perea, these requests exposed Hispanics to Pueblo practices steeped in native ceremony and religious tradition. On March 25, 1631, Ana Cadimo testified that at some time in 1629 she had approached a Tewa woman from San Ildefonso named Francisca Latiphaña in the hope of acquiring relief from a chronic ailment. Known for her experience in dealing with peyote, Latiphaña provided Cadimo with a cup containing a mixture of herbs dissolved in water. Before allowing Cadimo to drink the liquid, the curandera performed some unspecified chants and incantations. After drinking the concoction, Cadimo saw visions in the cup and imagined hearing music and what she thought were voices.

Although she did not comment on the efficacy of the therapy, it is interesting to note that in the same testimony Cadimo admitted to having approached a number of Pueblos a year later, again claiming to be in need of relief. She was told that she had been bewitched from quarters unknown and was given instructions to find an old Keres Indian from San Marcos. This medicine man, her native sources claimed, would provide her with enough peyote to cure her ills and enable her to visualize the person who had bewitched her. Cadimo followed the instructions but again declined to comment on their effectiveness during Perea's interrogation. As a postscript, Cadimo noted that at the time of her testimony the curandera who originally gave her peyote in 1629 continued to sell the drug to people of Santa Fe, promoting it now as a means of seeing great distances and identifying persons as they approached New Mexico along the camino real.[29]

More often, however, Hispanic settlers turned in their search for potions and cure-alls to the most convenient source of Pueblo knowledge—native relatives, household servants, and casual acquaintances. In June 1631, Juana de los Reyes testified that in order to halt her husband's extramarital affair she had approached a Keres woman serving in the household of Captain Diego de Santa Cruz for advice. The woman's recommendation was simple: "Take the urine of your husband's mistress and mix it with dog manure," she told de los Reyes, "and with that your husband and the woman will come to hate one another and he will continue to love you."[30] In a similar predicament in 1629, María Márquez sought the council of Alonso Gutiérrez's sister-in-law, a Tewa named Isabel Quagua. This time the instructions called for Márquez to take her husband's urine, mix it with unspecified herbs, and smear the potion on the doorstep of the man's new lover. This, the Tewa claimed, would sour the illicit romance.[31] Both women admitted to carrying out the instructions, but apparently neither remedy accomplished the desired effect.

Similarly, on November 4, 1661, María de Abisu testified that twenty-four years earlier, while in the company of her sister-in-law, doña María de Abedaño, the two women encountered an acquaintance of Abedaño's, an Indian from San Cristóbal named Pablo. Troubled by an unrequited love,

> the aforesaid Doña María de Abedaño asked [Abisu], as a person who understood the language of the Indian, to tell him to give her some herbs which would cause a man to love her very much and never forget her. The deponent went away to the garden, leaving the Indian and the aforesaid Doña María de Abedaño alone together; but she does not know what they said. . . . She does know that the Indian gave her the herbs . . . and that the woman is now married to the same man.[32]

Hispanic exposures to indigenous customs in New Mexico were not limited to the Pueblos, though; settlers also accepted and actively participated in ceremonial rites performed by the region's Athapaskan nomads. One documented example survives from 1660. In August of that year, Governor López de Mendizábal sent Diego Romero, alcalde ordinario of the villa of Santa Fe, and five other men to trade for buffalo hides and antelope skins among the Jicarilla Apaches on the Great Plains. Upon reaching the encampment of one Apache group, Romero exchanged pleasantries with the Indians and "asked them if they did not remember his father . . . [giving] them to understand by signs that he was a ruddy man who had come at such and such a time . . . and that he had left a son with an Indian woman among those Heathen, and that he himself was going to leave another." A long discussion among the Apaches ensued, which culminated in a ceremony later described by an eyewitness:

> At about four in the afternoon they brought a tent of new leather and set it up in the field; they then brought two bundles, one of antelope skins, and the other of buffalo skins, which they placed near the tent. Then they brought another large new buffalo skin which they stretched on the ground and put Diego Romero upon it, lying on his back. They then began to dance the *catzina*, making turns, singing, and raising up and laying Diego Romero

down again on the skin in accordance with the movement of the dance of the catzina. When the dance was ended about nightfall, they put him again on the skin, and taking it by the corners, drew him into the tent, into which they brought him a maiden, whom they left with him the entire night. On the next day in the morning the captains of the rancherias came to see whether Diego Romero had known the woman carnally; seeing that he had known her, they anointed Diego Romero's breast with the blood. They then put a feather on his head, in his hair, and proclaimed him as their captain.[33]

Countless numbers of similar testimonies fill the Inquisition documents from this period in New Mexico's history. Together, they paint a picture of the day-to-day lives of Hispanics in the northern colony, evoking images of an uneventful and rustic existence broken only by rumors and excited gossip about illicit affairs, failed romances, and perceived lapses into nativism and superstitious practices among neighbors, friends, or relatives. Perea himself, in carrying out his charge as commissary of the Holy Office, lamented what he judged to be the backwardness of the colony and decried the frequency with which its nonaboriginal inhabitants, "simple people [who] had no proper fear of [native] powders [and] herbs," displayed only a minimal comprehension of the teachings of the Catholic church.[34]

More importantly, however, these testimonies freeze for the historical record a dynamic that slowly eroded the cultural barrier separating Pueblo and European worlds. This process of acculturation would prove crucial to undercutting Spanish political authority in the region over the course of the seventeenth century. By 1680, New Mexico had become a backwash relative to the mainstream of Spanish-American colonial society, as Pueblos and Athapaskans wrought deep ethnic and cultural changes on the small European community over four generations. All vestiges of Oñate's dialectic of domination through physical distance and cultural segregation had vanished. Now a person of familiarity and even intimacy with the Pueblos, the Hispanic's position of authority stood in jeopardy.

Notes

1. The Muster Roll, January 8, 1598, in *Don Juan de Oñate, Colonizer of New Mexico, 1595–1628,* ed. and trans. George P. Hammond and Agapito Ray, 2 vols. (Albuquerque: University of New Mexico Press, 1953), 1:289. (Hereafter *Oñate.*)

2. Manifest of Don Luis de Velasco, in *Historical Documents Relating to New Mexico, Nueva Vizcaya, and Approaches Thereto, to 1773,* ed. Charles Wilson Hackett, trans. Adolph F. A. and Fanny R. Bandelier, 3 vols. (Washington, D.C.: Carnegie Institution, 1937), 1:429–33. (Hereafter *Documents.*)

3. First Hearing of Nicolás de Aguilar, Mexico, April 12, 1663, *Documents* 3:139.

4. Ibid.

5. Valverde Inspection, Espinosa Testimony, July 28, 1601, *Oñate* 2:638.

6. Fray Esteban de Perea, January 27, 1632, in France V. Scholes, Transcripts of documents housed in the Archivo General de la Nación Mexicana, Sección de la Inquisición (Library of Congress, Manuscript Division, Washington, D.C.). (Hereafter *Inquisición, Tom. 372,* AGN (Scholes transcript, Box 4615).

7. As quoted in France V. Scholes, *Troublous Times in New Mexico, 1659–1670* (Albuquerque: Historical Society of New Mexico Publications in History, 1942), p. 228.

8. Ibid., p. 223.

9. Ibid., p. 308.

10. Ibid., p. 7; and Fray Juan Bernal to the Tribunal, April, 1, 1669, *Documents* 3:270.

11. Ibid., p. 7; and Hearing of December 10, 1665, *Documents* 3:265.

12. Scholes, *Troublous Times,* p. 7; Fray Juan Bernal to the Tribunal, April 1, 1669, *Documents* 3:270; and Declaration of Joseph Nieto, January 19, 1667, *Documents* 3:272.

13. Scholes, *Troublous Times,* p. 7; and Letter from the Governor and Captain General, Don Antonio de Otermín, September 8, 1680, *Documents* 3:334.

14. Reply of Mendizabal, *Documents* 3:217.

15. Fray Alonso de Posadas to the Holy Office, May 23, 1662, *Documents* 3:149.

16. Deposition of Nicolás de Aguilar, May 8, 1663, *Documents* 3:171.

17. Ibid.

18. See chapter 5 of *The Pueblo Revolt of 1680.*

19. *Fray Alonso de Benavides' Revised Memorial of 1634,* ed. and trans. George P. Hammond (Albuquerque: University of New Mexico Press, 1945), p. 98.

20. The Valverde Investigation, Horta Testimony, July 30, 1601, in Hammond and Rey, *Oñate* 2:655.

21. Fray Estevan de Perea, November 10, 1631, *Inquisición, Tom. 372,* AGN (Scholes transcripts, Box 4615).

22. The 1631 contract for the supply of the New Mexico missions listed some provisions under the specific title of "For the Infirmary" (see Viceregal Decree Concerning the Contract, April 13, 1631, in Scholes, "Mission Supply," p. 101). Hints that this infirmary was located in the mission at San Felipe surface in a 1744 description of that pueblo: "Prior to the uprising of the year 1680 [the convent] was situated on the summit of a hill. . . . This convent, at the time of its erection, was the general hospital of the *custodia,* where the missionary religious and other persons were treated when they were ill" (Declaration of Fray Miguel de Menchero, Santa Bárbara, May 10, 1744, in *Documents* 3:394).

23. Of the 81,000 pesos spent in Mexico City to outfit the supply train bound for the northern missions in 1629, 1,200 went to the acquisition of various drugs and medicinal preserves. See Lansing B. Bloom, "Fray Estevan de Perea's *Relación,*" *New Mexico Historical Review* 8:3 (July 1933), p. 220.

24. Viceregal Decree Concerning the Contract, April 13, 1631, in Scholes, "Mission Supply," p. 101.

25. Testimony of Petronilla de Zamora, March 25, 1631, *Inquisición, Tom. 372,* AGN (Scholes Transcript, Box 4615): "havia oido desir esta declarante que [de los Angeles] era echisera de compacion . . ."

26. Testimony of Catalina Bernal, March 25, 1631, *Inquisición, Tom. 372,* AGN (Scholes transcripts, Box 4615).

27. See, for instance, the testimonies of Ana Cadimo (March 25, 1631), Juana Sánchez (June 22, 1631), and Catalina Bernal (March 26, 1631), *Inquisición,*

Tom. 372, AGN (Scholes transcripts, Box 4615). Sánchez testified that de los Angeles had given her the prescription as early as 1620, while others admitted to following the mestiza's advice in the later part of the decade.

28. Testimony of Catalina de Bustillos, March 26, 1631, *Inquisición, Tom. 372*, AGN (Scholes transcripts, Box 4615).

29. Testimony of Ana Cadimo, March 25, 1631, *Inquisición, Tom. 372*, AGN (Scholes transcripts, Box 4615): "Ana Cadimo . . . dice y denuncia . . . q un año poco mas o menos q diciendile los indios . . . que estaba enechisada y q tomase el peiote i con el veria a quien le avia enechisado y hecho mal, q viendolo sanaria luego y veria tambien el echiso y donde estaba y . . . q buscase un indio q se lo diese y asi busco un indio biejo de san marcos de nacion qres el qual tomo lio i dio vever con un poco de agua a esta declarante. . . . Dice mas esta declarante q abra dos o tres años q una india tegua del pueblo de S. ildefonso llamada francisca latiphaña le dio a vever otras ierbas desechas en un jumate de agua . . . pero primero que la india se lo diese a vever asia algunas seremonias i conjuros y contaba y . . . q via en algunos visiones en el agua . . . y asia la musica y ablaba. . . . No sabe otra cosa mas de q agora dos años esta mesma india . . . se desia publicamente en esta villa q avia tomado el peiote para ver quien venia de tierra de pas."

30. Testimony of Juana de los Reyes, June 21, 1631, *Inquisición, Tom. 372*, AGN (Scholes transcripts, Box 4615).

31. Testimony of Juana Sánchez, June 22, 1631, *Inquisición, Tom. 372*, AGN (Scholes transcripts, Box 4615).

32. Denunciation by María de Abisu, Santa Fe, November 4, 1661, in Hackett, *Documents* 3:183.

33. Testimony of Nicolás de Freitas, January 25, 1661, *Documents* 3:161. See also John L. Kessell, "Diego Romero, the Plains Apaches, and the Inquisition," *The American West* 15 (May–June 1978), pp. 12–16.

34. Fray Esteban de Perea, November 10, 1631, *Inquisición, Tom. 372*, AGN (Scholes transcripts, Box 4615).

Making Connections

We end where we began, with questions. Each of the selections addresses some if not all of the questions that follow. The answers to these questions might have seemed straightforward after reading a single selection, but they become more complicated after comparing the work of several scholars who have approached the subject with different abilities, sensibilities, questions, and methods. This variety of approach is in the nature of the way that historians work. Some historians dig more deeply and find better evidence than do other historians; in the end, evidence matters. Some historians read the evidence more shrewdly or knowledgeably than other historians and construct wiser answers. Sometimes historians merely have different but equally valid answers because there are many ways to understand the human condition, past as well as present.

Your own responses to the readings have their own validity, and if you answer these questions with more questions you will be doing what good historians do.

1. What was the primary reason that Pueblos revolted after so many years of coexistence with Spaniards? Which of the selections agree on this point? Which disagree?

2. What were the secondary reasons? Which of the selections agree? Which disagree?

3. We could think of competing explanations of the Pueblo Revolt as falling into two main camps: those who argue that Pueblos and Spaniards developed a mutually beneficial relationship before exterior forces tore them apart in the 1660s and 1670s and those who see a long-standing antagonistic relationship made worse by the events of the 1660s and 1670s. Which of the writers you have read falls into the first camp? Which the second? Do any of the writers fall in between?

4. Bowden and Gutiérrez see religious oppression as a primary cause of the revolt, but they offer very different insights. What do you see as the principal difference between their interpretations?

5. Which selection or selections best explain how Pueblos achieved sufficient unity to overcome the distances and language barriers that divided their autonomous towns? Why?

6. Chávez and Knaut consider the role of mixed bloods in the coming of the revolt but see them playing different roles. Compare their arguments and explain which you find most convincing.

7. Several of the selections suggest that Pueblos and Spaniards found much in common, but they describe those commonalities in different ways and as having different effects. Compare them.

8. Wouldn't it be better if historians agreed with one another?

Suggestions for Further Reading

This volume is not intended to provide a massive bibliography, but any interested student will want to delve into the subject more deeply. For a selection drawn from a book, the best way to start is to go to that book and place the selection within the author's larger argument. Each selection is reproduced with full annotation, as originally published, to allow intensely interested students to go to the author's original sources, study them, and compare their own readings with what the author has made of the same material.

The significance and drama of the Pueblo Revolt have made it the subject of several well-written books. Andrew L. Knaut, *The Pueblo Revolt of 1680: Conquest and Resistance in Seventeenth-Century New Mexico* (Norman: University of Oklahoma Press, 1995), supersedes Robert Silverberg, *The Pueblo Revolt* (New York: Weybright and Talley, 1970), and its bibliography is the starting place for further research. Franklin Folsom, *Red Power on the Rio Grande: The Native American Revolution of 1680*, introduction by Alfonso Ortiz (1973; reprint, Albuquerque: University of New Mexico Press, 1996), is a sprightly, brief account for young readers, written with deep sympathy for Pueblo culture. These books are all indebted to Charles Wilson Hackett, ed., *Revolt of the Pueblo Indians of New Mexico and Otermín's Attempted Reconquest, 1680–1682*, trans. Charmion Clair Shelby, 2 vols. (Albuquerque: University of New Mexico Press, 1942), which contains translations of the key documents. Sources essential to understanding a second large-scale Pueblo Revolt can be found in J. Manuel Espinosa, ed. and trans., *The Pueblo Indian Revolt of 1696 and the Franciscan Missions in New Mexico: Letters of the Missionaries and Related Documents* (Norman: University of Oklahoma Press, 1988).

For a vivid introduction to Pueblo culture and scholars' disagreements about how to understand it, see the opening chapter of Ramón A. Gutiérrez, *When Jesus Came, the Corn Mothers Went Away: Marriage, Sexuality, and Power in New Mexico, 1500–1846* (Stanford: Stanford University Press, 1991), and its critics: Ted Jojola et al., "Commentaries: *When Jesus Came, the Corn Mothers Went Away: Marriage, Sex, and Power in New Mexico, 1500–1846,* by Ramón Gutiérrez," *American Indian Culture and Research Journal* 17 (1993):

141–77, and Sylvia Rodríguez, "Subaltern Historiography on the Rio Grande: On Gutiérrez's *When Jesus Came, the Corn Mothers Went Away,*" *American Ethnologist* 21 (1994): 892–99.

Carroll L. Riley, *Rio del Norte, People of the Upper Rio Grande from Earliest Times to the Pueblo Revolt* (Salt Lake City: University of Utah Press, 1995), is particularly useful for Pueblo prehistory. Joe S. Sando, *The Pueblo Indians* (San Francisco: Indian Historian Press, 1976), represents a synthesis of the Pueblo past by an Indian historian from Jémez Pueblo. The richest and most vividly written study of a single pueblo in the Spanish era is John L. Kessell, *Kiva, Cross, and Crown: The Pecos Indians and New Mexico* (Washington, D.C.: National Park Service, 1979). Oakah L. Jones Jr., *Pueblo Warriors and Spanish Conquest* (Norman: University of Oklahoma Press, 1966), emphasizes Spanish-Pueblo military cooperation. Jack D. Forbes, *Apache, Navaho, and Spaniard* (1960; reprint, Norman: University of Oklahoma Press, 1994), examines Pueblo relations with their Athapaskan neighbors, some of them nomads. At the time they were published in 1960 and 1966, the works of Forbes and Jones gave uncommon attention to the roles of Indians as historical actors and stood out amidst a Eurocentric literature on the Hispanic Southwest.

Gutiérrez, *When Jesus Came,* also offers a fine synthesis of Franciscan belief and practice and a richly detailed portrayal of life in Hispanic New Mexico in the seventeenth century. His work, only a small portion of which is excerpted in this reader, takes us a step beyond the pioneering studies by France Scholes, whose painstaking archival research gave us the first detailed look at life in seventeenth-century New Mexico — particularly its pathologies. Much of Scholes's still-essential writing on New Mexico appeared serially in article form in the 1930s and then was reprinted as monographs: France V. Scholes, *Church and State in New Mexico, 1610–1650,* Historical Society of New Mexico, Publications in History, vol. 7 (Albuquerque: University of New Mexico Press, 1937); France V. Scholes, *Troublous Times in New Mexico, 1659–1670,* Historical Society of New Mexico, Publications in History, vol. 11 (Albuquerque: University of New Mexico Press, 1942). William H. Broughton, "The History of Seventeenth-Century New Mexico: Is It Time for New Interpretations?" *New Mexico Historical Review* 68 (1993): 3–12, asserts but does not convincingly demonstrate that Scholes favored clerics over civil officials and overemphasized church-state conflict. For an anthropologist's view of the Franciscans' blinders, see Daniel T. Reff, "The 'Predicament of Culture' and Spanish Missionary Accounts of the Tepehuan and Pueblo Revolts," *Ethnohistory* 42 (Winter 1995): 63–90. John L. Kessell, "Restoring Seventeenth-Century New Mexico, Then and Now," *Society for Historical Archaeology* 31 (1997): 46–54, masterfully synthesizes current literature, both archaeological and historical.

In the seventeenth century, New Mexico and Florida were the only Spanish colonies located in the area of the present-day United States (Spaniards did not move into California, Arizona, Texas, or Louisiana until the eighteenth century). For New Mexico in the context of Hispanic activity in what is now the United States, see David J. Weber, *The Spanish Frontier in North America* (New Haven: Yale University Press, 1992).

Students interested in thinking more deeply about how historians have explained white-Indian relations in what is now the United States could do no better than consult Kerwin Lee Klein, *Frontiers of the Imagination: Narrating the European Conquest of Native America, 1890–1990* (Berkeley: University of California Press, 1997), and Devon Mihesuah, ed., *Natives and Academics: Researching and Writing about American Indians* (Lincoln: University of Nebraska Press, 1998).